YOU,
PROPERTY
and your
PENSION

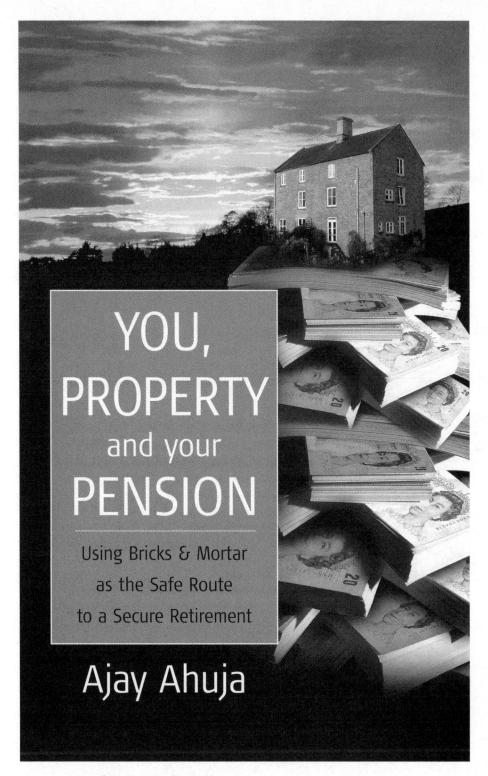

YOU, PROPERTY and your PENSION

Using Bricks & Mortar as the Safe Route to a Secure Retirement

Ajay Ahuja

howtobooks

Published by How To Books Ltd
3 Newtec Place, Magdalen Road
Oxford, OX4 1RE, United Kingdom
Tel: (01865) 793806. Fax: (01865) 248780
email: info@howtobooks.co.uk
www.howtobooks.co.uk

British Library Cataloguing in Publication Data
A catalogue record for this book is available from the British Library

Cover design by Baseline Arts Ltd, Oxford
Produced for How To Books by Deer Park Productions, Tavistock
Typeset by TW Typesetting, Plymouth, Devon
Printed and bound in Great Britain by Bell & Bain Ltd, Glasgow

NOTE: The material contained in this book is set out in good faith for general
guidance and no liability can be accepted for loss or expense incurred as a
result of relying in particular circumstances on statements made in this book.
Laws and regulations may be complex and liable to change, and readers
should check the current position with the relevant authorities before making
personal arrangements.

Contents

I dedicate this book to my mother

Special thanks to Giles and Nikki, my family and Ellie

For further information on the property market you can subscribe to *www.propertyhotspots.net* for up to the minute information on property hotspots, property prices, property search, estate agents, letting agents, property auctions, 100% mortgage providers, buy to let mortgage providers and much more.

Introduction

Let me tell you the key findings of a major investment bank's survey released on 22 September 2003:

◆ Only 1 in 4 workers is set to retire on a pension greater than half their salary.

◆ This means that 3 out of 4 workers will retire on half their salary or less.

◆ 1 in 2 workers will retire on less than 40% of their final salary.

Can you afford to live on half your salary in today's terms? Or 40% in today's terms?

The reason for this is that the stock market has not performed as expected. Annuity rates have declined due to people living longer and the situation is only going to get worse with the increasing quality of health care.

Seven years ago at the age of 24 I initially invested in property to provide myself with a pension. The main reasons I did this were:

◆ I didn't trust *anyone* handling my hard-earned cash apart from myself.

◆ I thought it was morally wrong for a pension company to take my money and not allow me to have access to it until I was of retirement age.

The funny thing is that even though I invested in property initially to provide myself with a retirement income, I found that my property income was in excess of my salary so I was able to retire at the age of 27! Now I own a portfolio of 75 properties that earn me an income now, into retirement and beyond.

When you contribute to a pension fund you are investing in a business (by way of shares) that you have no control of. If the managing director decides to go on a mad shopping spree and bleed the company dry you have no recourse. The director may go to jail but you won't get your money back. Just have a look at some of the high profile cases – WorldCom, Enron, etc. And these are only the ones that hit the press. There are companies that you probably will not have heard of that a pension fund company invests in and may have suffered the same problems but on a smaller scale.

Property is something you do have control of. It's yours! You don't own a piece of paper called a share certificate. You own something you can see, touch and do with whatever pleases you. But simply owning property is not your route to retirement bliss. You need to know how to exploit the opportunities that ownership brings.

The difference between property and any other investment is the ability to borrow. You can borrow to purchase the property and let the tenant pay your interest payments by way of rent – hence it's a self-funding investment. It is true that you can borrow to buy shares but the dividends you will receive are rarely sufficient to cover the loan repayments. Also, the maximum any bank will lend you will be up to 50% of the value of the shares, and the interest rate is much higher than a typical mortgage because shares are riskier than property. This begs the question – if shares are riskier than property why do people invest in shares rather than property?

Well, there are some answers to this question. Apart from the tax breaks you get which make investing in pension funds seemingly tax efficient, we invest in shares because:

- We are lazy! It's easier to simply pay over some money and let someone else do the hard work.

- Other people do! We act like sheep sometimes and follow the crowd. If others are doing it we'll do it too.

- We are too trusting of these big pension companies. We fall for their mock caring TV adverts, glossy spreads in the national newspapers and magazines, and impressive head offices and branches.

So it's time to take up the profession of a landlord and start enjoying the rewards that have been enjoyed by the middle class for centuries – it's time to build that property pension!

If, after reading this book, you find it has not taken you far enough and you need further help in building your property pension then please contact me at:

Web: www.buytolethotspots.com

Fax: 01277 362563

Email: emergencyaccountants@yahoo.co.uk

Address: Accountants Direct, 99 Moreton Road, Ongar,
Essex, CM5 0AR

I wish you the best of luck with your future property purchases.

Ajay Ahuja

Traditional Pension *v.* Property Pension

Pensions are a numbers game.

But it's not about how much you put away for retirement. You can contribute heavily to a pension investment fund and it can return you very little in the long term – no matter how many tax breaks, frills or top-ups you receive. There is no come-back or guarantee – it's your loss! These tax breaks, frills and top-ups are there to entice you to invest in companies which prop up our economy but have no real strategy to provide *you* with a real long-term income that is related to your lifestyle or even your contributions.

I can already hear you say – what a cynic! But if you understand the principles involved you may change your opinion. I am going to show you in words, pictures and numbers how property is a better way to invest for your retirement than any other method. It's important to understand why:

1. The Government, pension companies and the banks *cannot* deliver you a guaranteed long-term income sufficient for a comfortable life.

2. Property *can* deliver an income for you, *your family and your subsequent family members* that is far in excess of what any of the above can do.

You may think this is a tall order. But if you take the time to really understand how long-term income is created you will realise that my first statement that pensions is a numbers game, is true, and you will laugh at what is currently offered to you as a 'pension' from a traditional pension provider.

TRADITIONAL PENSION PROVIDERS

There are three broad categories of traditional pension providers:

1. The Government
2. Pension companies
3. The banks

We are now going to look at what is so bad about the traditional providers. Let's look at what they offer.

The Government

The Government offers you a state pension. You will get this whether you like it or not. You contribute, via your National Insurance contributions which are deducted at source or, if you are self-employed, deducted from your profits twice a year. The contribution is capped and when you come to retirement the Government pays a pension currently of around £300 per month. This equates to 9% to 20% of the average UK annual salary, depending on where you live in the country.

Even though the Government offers a debatable value on your contributions, being only £300 per month from full service, a state pension is something we cannot avoid so it's not worth applauding it or rubbishing it as there is nothing we can do about it!

Another incentive the Government offers is a contribution to a pension fund *if* you contribute to a pension fund. The contribution is paid by way of not having to pay tax. So if you earn £2,000 per month and pay £200 to a pension company then your taxable income is £1,800, being your income less your pension contribution. If you are a basic rate tax payer, then you will save $21\% \times £200 = £42$ on tax. This is then expressed as an additional contribution by the Government in that if you didn't contribute you would have only got £158 out of the £200. So it's a contribution of £158 from you and £42 from the Government.

If you're a 40% tax rate payer the Government contribution is even bigger! In the above example it would be a £120 contribution from you and £80 from the Government – quite an incentive on the face of it.

But what is the Government allowing you to contribute to? It is not giving you this money to put away or to invest for your future. It is saying you can contribute to something that only the Government agrees with – its economy!

This has a double effect. First, it means there is investment in the UK economy which helps our UK-based economies grow and increases the tax collected from these UK companies.

Second, it forces the man on the street to take a *risk* on their retirement income rather than have the Government take the risk. If the pension fund doesn't grow to the desired level then that's just your misfortune. The Government has given you a big incentive to invest in a pension fund but carries no responsibility if your pension fund is worth zero! To be fair to the Government it's not a bad trade off. It loses anywhere between 21%–40% of your salary, in tax, to mitigate the risk of having to provide for you in the future.

Pension companies

So the Government has given you a tax break of up to 40% – what do the pension companies offer you? Well, they offer you no guarantees, that's for sure. What they will do however is, take your money, charge you a fee for doing so, invest it in companies that they have no control over and hope to return you an amount greater than a building society would. The reality is that in the last 5 years you would have been lucky to get any profit at all! The stock market is very risky even if it is managed by a pension company. You'd have been better off investing in a building society or bank. See next section.

Please disregard past growth rates of the stock market. Quite impressively the stock market has outperformed every investment out there in the past 50 years apart from the last 10. This is why people have assumed that it is so safe, but you must never assume that the past = the future. The stock market has changed dramatically in the way people invest, the type of companies listed, the fluidity in which the market moves and the legislation governing these companies. Dramatic gains are likely to be a thing of the past as most of the gains occurred during the last 50 years.

The banks

If I were to recommend a pension fund other than property then I would recommend a good old deposit account with an established bank or building society. If you want to retire with peace of mind knowing that you will have at least something to live on then this is the safest way. The problem is you have to contribute so much to even come close to an income that will match your current salary that it seems an impossible task. There are no tax advantages to following this route and the rates the bank pay are so incredibly low that it doesn't even seem worth bothering.

Also if you look at any pension fund you will see that they have cash reserves. The trend has been lately to keep most of these funds in cash – and they charge you an annual management fee to do so! This results in the poor performance of the pension fund due to their charges and the lower returns to be had from cash. You have to ask yourself – why pay a pension company to put your money in to a cash reserve when you can do it yourself *and* for free! You'll probably get a better rate than them as well.

HOW A TRADITIONAL PENSION AND A PROPERTY PENSION WORK

The only real competitor to a property pension is a pension offered by a pension company. So it makes sense to look into how both these pensions work and how they compare. Can I warn you that the numbers get quite complex if you're not that numerate. I've tried to keep it as simple as possible, so bear with me. I guess the reason why so many people have been duped by the pension companies is because of this very fact! It is easy to get blinded by the science.

Let's look at a traditional pension.

Traditional pension

Joe is 41. He works in an office earning £30,000 per year and is a basic rate tax payer. He decides to take out a private pension. He comes across a reputable firm offering:

Management Fee   1%
Estimated Growth   5%

A management fee is the charge a pension company makes for managing your money. This seems reasonable from their side as no one would do this for nothing. They invest your money in so called 'safe' investments such as cash deposits, bonds and shares. Some pension fund managers are very good at what they do (even though they are an exception) and are well worth their charge as they can out-perform the general market.

Estimated growth is how much the fund manager thinks he can make your money grow. If current rates offered by building societies are 2.5% then a 5% growth is very attractive as it is double what is being offered from a bank or building society. If you take into account the tax breaks then it seems even more attractive.

Let's assume that the pension company actually achieves their estimated growth target of 5% year on year. If Joe invested £100 per month, increasing his contribution by 4.25% year on year, his personal contribution, government contribution and fund value would be:

Age	Personal contribution	Government contribution (tax)	Value of year's contribution at age 65
41	1,200	252	4,868
42	1,251	263	4,833
43	1,304	274	4,799
44	1,360	286	4,764
45	1,417	298	4,730
46	1,478	310	4,696
47	1,540	323	4,663
48	1,606	337	4,630
49	1,674	352	4,597
50	1,745	367	4,564

51	1,819	382	4,531
52	1,897	398	4,499
53	1,977	415	4,467
54	2,061	433	4,435
55	2,149	451	4,403
56	2,240	470	4,372
57	2,336	490	4,340
58	2,435	511	4,309
59	2,538	533	4,279
60	2,646	556	4,248
61	2,759	579	4,218
62	2,876	604	4,188
63	2,998	630	4,158
64	3,126	656	4,128
65	3,258	684	4,098
Total	**51,690**	10,854	**111,817**

So Joe's pension fund at his chosen age of retirement, 65, is £111,817. Then Joe has to purchase an annuity, which is a guaranteed annual income till his death, with his pension fund. AXA Sunlife offer £45.78 annual income for every £1,000. So Joe's annual income in retirement is:

£45.78 × £111,817/1,000 = **£5,118.98 p.a.** (say £5,119)

Figure 1 provides an illustration of this.

Now let me draw your attention to two key figures – what you put in and what you get out:

What you put in	Total pension contributions for the 25 years	£51,690
What you get out	Annual income from the annuity till death	£5,119 p.a. till death

These should really be the only two figures you should be interested in. These two key figures can only ever be the most important figures

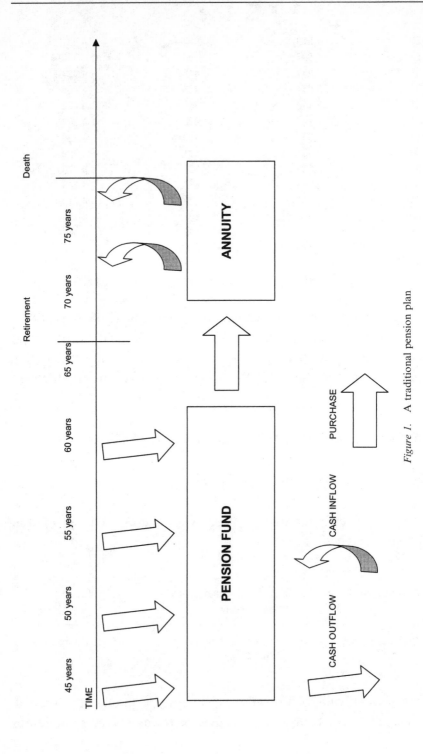

Figure 1. A traditional pension plan

in the whole pension equation. In fact, these two figures are always the key indicators whenever a business person appraises the likely success of a potential investment. A pension fund is an investment so there should be no other way of looking at its performance.

What you put in is totally **within** your control. Therefore this number is known. It is for you to decide how much you should put away for your retirement. You can be advised on how much you should put away but no one can guarantee what you'll get out of it. However, you can be assured that most sane people want to put the least away for the most gain.

What you get out is totally **out of** your control. Unless you have taken out a guaranteed benefit pension (which guarantees a fraction of your final salary, usually two-thirds) which is hugely expensive and normally only available to executive directors, you will have no idea what your pension fund and thus your annual income will be. You can only ever estimate what you'll get out, with the accuracy of your estimation increasing as you get closer to the maturity date.

So in the above traditional pension Joe put in £51,692 and he's got out £5,119 p.a. He may get £1,000 p.a. or he may get £10,000 p.a. depending on the performance of his pension fund. But at 5% growth rates he has got roughly **10%** of his contributions as an annual income, being £51,690 contributions and £5,119 annual income. Now we can't say that's good or bad unless we have an alternative to compare it with.

Now let's look at a property pension. More importantly – what you put in and what you get out.

Property pension
So what's a property pension? Well, the name suggests it all! It's a fund invested in property that delivers an income from the rent derived from these properties. In other words, retirement income

from rent. But why is a property pension better than a traditional pension? It has nothing to do with the past. It's to do with the present and the future. If we were to get in to a game of how pension funds have outperformed property or the other way round then we would go nowhere. The reason for this is because it's historic. Look at the following table:

Return	Pensions[1]	Property[2]
Over 5 years	11%	92%
Over 10 years	61%	142%
Over 15 years	191%	156%
Over 20 years	441%	358%

[1]Average individual pension: income reinvested. Figures do not include tax relief. Source: Standard and Poor's.
[2]Average UK house price. Source: Nationwide.

Both pensions have done well but it depends on which time frame you look at. Over 15 and 20 years pension funds win but over 5 and 10 years property wins! So it depends on what time frame you look at. The only common thing between these figures is that they all happened in the past. The only people who benefited from these are the people who made these investments. The key to understanding how you can always win with property is to understand the concept of gearing. Or in other words having the ability to borrow.

The mortgage market has changed dramatically. It is now possible to buy a property with the lender's money based on the rental income only. So you are not expected to earn a certain salary to obtain a buy-to-let mortgage of up to £500,000. The only problem is you need a larger deposit compared to the traditional 5% deposit for a residential mortgage. The least you need is 15% deposit but in some cases you need 30%. Because of the introduction of the buy-to-let mortgage, house prices have risen way above wage inflation rates. This is because property prices are now determined by the rental value of the home rather than its desirability.

So let's look at the cashflows. Jill is 41. She works in an office earning £30,000 per year and is a basic rate tax payer. She decides to build a property pension. She can afford to save £100 per month to build a deposit and buy a property costing £30,000. She can rent it out for £2,400 per year which equates to 8% of the purchase price, i.e. 8% yield. She decides to buy a property every time she saves up enough for a deposit.

Now I'm going to have to hold your hand through these figures! Jill buys four properties over the 25 years with property values rising 5% every year (the same growth rate as the pension fund). She rents them out and allows a 20% loss of rent due to agent's fees, void periods and repairs. Allowing for this she gets an annual profit rising every time she buys a property and allowing for rent inflation (applied every five years). So the annual profits after tax (basic rate 21% – expected for 2005) are calculated from the following table:

Property		1	2	3	4	
	Yrs 0–5	Yrs 6–10	Yrs 11–15	Yrs 16–20	Yrs 21–25	Yrs 26 onwards
Purchase price		30,000				
Deposit (15% of purchase price)		4,500				
Debt		25,500				
Rent (8% yield)		2,400	3,063	3,909	4,989	6,368
Interest (5% APR)		1,275	1,275	1,275	1,275	1,275
Other costs (20% of rent)		480	613	782	998	1,274
Net inflow before tax		645	1,175	1,852	2,717	3,819
After tax (21% basic rate)		510	929	1,463	2,146	3,017
Fees		1,500				
Total deposit and fees		6,000				
Purchase price			38,288			
Deposit (15% of purchase price)			5,743			
Debt			32,545			
Rent (8% yield)			3,063	3,909	4,989	6,368
Interest (5% APR)			1,627	1,627	1,627	1,627
Other costs (20% of rent)			613	782	998	1,274

Property	1	2	3	4
Net inflow before tax		823	1,500	2,364	3,467
After tax (21% Basic rate)		650	1,185	1,868	2,739
Fees			2,000		
Total deposit and fees			7,743		
Purchase price			48,867		
Deposit (15% of purchase price)			7,330		
Debt			41,537		
Rent (8% yield)			3,909	4,989	6,368
Interest (5% APR)			2,077	2,077	2,078
Other costs (20% of rent)			782	998	1,274
Net inflow before tax			1,051	1,915	3,016
After tax (21% Basic rate)			830	1,512	2,383
Fees			2,500		
Total deposit and fees			9,830		
Purchase price				62,368	
Deposit (15% of purchase price)				9,355	
Debt				53,013	
Rent (8% yield)				4,989	6,368
Interest (5% APR)				2,651	2,651
Other costs (20% of rent)				998	1,274
Net inflow before tax				1,341	2,443
After tax (21% Basic rate)				1,059	1,930
Fees				3,000	
Total deposit and fees				12,355	
Annual profit inflow	510	1,579	3,479	6,586	10,070

Now, having calculated the figures above we can derive the key figures in building a comparison with a traditional pension. The key figures being:

- deposit and fees put down to acquire the properties
- the profits from these properties
- the purchase price of these properties
- the value of these properties at retirement
- the debt outstanding on these properties at retirement

Figure 2 provides an illustration of this.

Property	Age	Deposit and fees (outflow)	Profit (inflow)	Net outflow	Purchase price (5% growth p.a.)	Property value at age 65	Debt (mortgage)	Net Value
	41							
	42							
	43							
	44							
1	45	6,000			30,000	83,579	25,500	58,079
	46	0	510					
	47	0	510					
	48	0	510					
	49	0	510					
2	50	7,743	510		38,288	83,579	32,545	51,034
	51	0	1,579					
	52	0	1,579					
	53	0	1,579					
	54	0	1,579					
3	55	9,830	1,579		48,867	83,579	41,537	42,042
	56	0	3,479					
	57	0	3,479					
	58	0	3,479					
	59	0	3,479					
4	60	12,355	3,479		62,368	83,579	53,013	30,566
	61	0	6,586					
	62	0	6,586					
	63	0	6,586					
	64	0	6,586					
	65	0	6,586					
		35,928	**60,764**	**−24,836**	179,523	334,316	152,595	**181,721**

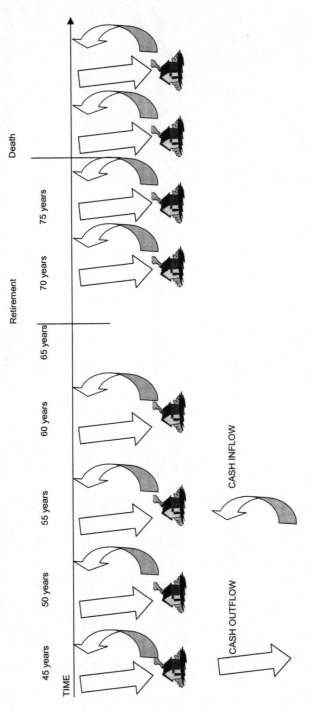

Figure 2. A property pension plan

So Jill's property pension fund is £181,721, being the value of the properties less the mortgage debt. But just like the traditional pension fund we have assumed a 5% growth in property prices. Now, I am not a fortune teller, so I have no idea what the growth rate will be averaged out over the next 25 years. Even though a property pension fund is *greater* than a traditional pension after tax at the same growth rates (£181,721 v £111,814) – the great thing is that IT DOESN'T MATTER!

So why doesn't it matter? The 5% growth is nice and probably realistic but it doesn't provide us with an income. What we're interested in is the rental income. The key figures you should be looking at are the two key figures I talked about earlier. Let me remind you – what you put in and what you get out! So here's what we've put in and what we've got out:

| What you put in | Deposit and fees less profits from the properties over the 25 years | − £24,836 |
| What you get out | Profits for years 26 onwards | £10,070 p.a. forever |

So with a property pension you actually get money back! What you put in is a negative amount. Your investment in property by way of deposits and fees is replenished by the profits made in property and more. Being prudent, let's assume that the profit just covers the deposit and fees only. This means that over the 25 years what you have put in is still only NIL!

So what have you got out of it? Well, a nice income of over £10,000 p.a. which is twice as much as what a traditional pension can offer. And this income is not just for your life but for your descendants after your death as the properties pass to your beneficiaries in your will.

If you do want a risk-free pension and want to purchase an annuity, then the net value of the properties does matter because you have to sell the properties. The beauty of property is that you can sell when you want to. So you can sell when the market is high or hold when the market is low. The market could be high enough to sell within 15 years of you making the first property purchase or you may have to wait 30 years. Assuming the property portfolio does perform at 5% growth p.a. then the net fund after tax will be:

Proceeds of property sales	**£334,316**
Purchase prices	£179,523
Profit	£154,793
Tax Relief	(£61,917)
Chargeable Gain	£92,876
@40%	£37,150

So net proceeds will be:

Proceeds of property sales	£334,316
Tax bill	(£37,150)
Net proceeds before mortgage debt	£297,166
Mortgage debt	(£152,595)
Net proceeds	**£144,571**

Using the same annuity rates as above of £45.78 per £1,000 the risk-free pension till death is:

£144,571 × £45.78/1,000 = £6,618.44 p.a.

COMPARISON TABLES

So let's look at a proper comparison table of the figures:

	Traditional pension	Property pension (buy and hold)	Property pension (buy and sell)
What you put in	£51,692	Nil	Nil
What you get out	£5,119 p.a. till death	£10,070 p.a. forever	£6,618.44 p.a. till death

I hope that you can clearly see that property pensions outperform traditional pensions quite astronomically even with all the tax breaks. This is because you essentially put no money in and get more out! Even if the traditional fund did return you a higher income, the property pension would win as you haven't put anything in!

This is why traditional pensions are a joke.

But it doesn't stop there! It's not only the numbers that make a good case for a property pension. There are other factors that make a property pension superior to a traditional pension which are in part drawn out from the figures above. Look at the table below.

	Traditional pension	Property pension
Flexibility	Pensions are inflexible by their very nature as you can't get hold of your cash until you are 50. Even then it's only 25% of the fund.	You can sell your property or properties when you want. So if the market is high or you need the cash, then the money can be unlocked relatively quickly whenever you want.
Longevity of income	The income from a pension stops when you die. Now this may not be a problem for you (because you're dead!) but this could be a problem for your dependants. You can get a pension that pays out to your spouse but you have to pay for it! The annuity rates are much lower.	The income streams carry on regardless of your death. Just because you die it doesn't mean your tenant has to stop paying rent. The rent will simply be paid to whoever you leave the property or properties to when you die. This is how some families have become very rich due to the inheritance of property from their ancestors.
Present income	There is no income stream until you purchase the annuity. This may be 40 years after you made the first payment into the pension fund.	When you invest in property you will get income straight away. If you've bought the right property then you will get an income even after paying out for the expenses such as the mortgage and repairs.
Instinctive	How do you choose a good pension fund? It's very hard to choose a good fund. You can use historic data but historic data tells you nothing about future performance. You have to take on the risk that your fund manager will do well with your money. How well he or she will do is	It's easier to pick a good house rather than a good stock or pension company. You will have an instinctive knowledge about property as we have all lived in one! It's something you can touch and feel rather than a paper statement sent to you once a year!

	Traditional pension	**Property pension**
	impossible to tell. You do not even get the chance to meet them!	
Income rises with inflation	If you purchase an annuity with a fixed income payout then you will receive a fixed amount till death. Your real income will diminish over time due to price inflation. The only way to counteract this is to take out an annuity that pays an income that rises with inflation. But you've guessed it – it costs! So the annuity rates are lower.	Rent rises with wage inflation at the very least. However, current demographics show that property is in short supply and the situation is set to get worse. Fragmenting families, increasing population, first-time buyers being priced out and building quotas not being met will cause rents to *probably* rise above inflation.
Gearing	You are unable to borrow to contribute to a pension fund as there will be no way you could service the loan repayments.	You are able to borrow because the lender takes first charge on the property and knows you can service the debt from the rent paid by the tenant. The potential growth of your property fund is magnified due to the growth being on the whole property price rather than the actual amount invested.
Known retirement income	You will have no idea what your retirement income will be. You can only make an estimation but it will depend heavily on the size of your fund and the annuity rates being offered at the time of retirement.	It's easier to predict your retirement income if you choose properties that give you an income you desire now. So, for example, if you require an income equivalent to your salary of £2,000 per month, then choose 4 properties that have a rental figure of £500 each. Then you can be assured that when you retire the rental figures would have risen roughly with inflation to provide you with a real income of £2,000 per month.
No cap on contributions	You are capped on the contributions to a pension fund to qualify for full tax relief. You can contribute further but you do lose out on all the tax benefits.	Because you have already factored in the lack of tax benefits in the whole equation then the amount you want to contribute is completely up to you.

Not relying on growth	The fund has to grow to a desired level for you to draw an income sufficient for your retirement. This is very difficult to predict as shown by all the pension companies offering these types of pensions.	Growth is nice but you are relying on rental income. Rent does not go down – it rises with inflation so you can be assured that the income derived from your properties will be sufficient and growth will be irrelevant. (This is only applicable for a buy and hold strategy.)
Annuity rates are always inferior to property yields	Annuity rates are very poor and will never exceed 8% for someone aged 65. This is because we live longer. In this example if they gave you 8% then they will expect you to die in 12.5 years. This is just under the average life expentancy of 79, being 77.5 years. They will give you an income based on you living till 90 and hope you die at 79! This equates to a 5% rate.	8% + yields are easily achievable – even though property prices are said to be at an all-time high. A list of over 350 areas are listed in the reference chapter that offer an 8% yield or greater. Thus property will always be a better investment than an annuity.
Risk and control	You place all the control with a fund manager. He is in full control of your money and exposes you fully to the risks that only he takes on.	You take the risks that you want. You are in full control of the decisions you wish to take. You are exposed exclusively to the risks only you wish to take.

ASSUMPTIONS

Now there have been a number of assumptions made in deriving these calculations. These are necessary otherwise we could not build a picture of your future income. Here are a list of the assumptions I have made for each type of pension, how reasonable they are and how relevant they are to the overall performance of each.

Traditional pension

Assumption	Reasonable?	Relevant to performance?
Basic rate tax payer	I have chosen Basic rate as I have assumed most people are Basic rate tax rate payers which is the case. In the appendix, however, is	Yes. A higher rate tax payer gets a higher retirement income than a Basic rate tax payer in a traditional pension example but they still

Assumption	Reasonable?	Relevant to performance?
	the calculation for a higher rate tax payer.	receive less than a property pension. So a property pension is still superior.
1% Management Fee	There are few if any that charge less than 1% and there are some that charge in excess of 1%. The industry norm for pension funds is 1%.	Because this is the industry standard it is a safe assumption so as not to distort the figures.
5% Growth of fund	This is a very difficult question as we are crystal ball gazing. We cannot base it on past performance as that is no indication. The key fact is that it is the same growth rate as the property calculations so neither has an advantage.	No, as both growth rates were set equal.
4.25% Growth in contributions	Would seem reasonable taking into account inflation and promotional pay increases.	No. As we have looked at the contributions in total over the 25 years the individual contributions over the years are broadly irrelevant as in both examples the contributions were spread out.
Start age of 41	The start age is not really relevant as the pensions were being compared.	No. Both start ages were the same.
Retirement age of 65	The retirement age is not really relevant as the pensions were being compared.	No. Both retirement ages were the same.

Property pension

Assumption	Reasonable?	Relevant to performance?
Basic rate tax payer	I have chosen Basic rate as I have assumed most people are Basic rate tax rate payers which is the case. In the appendix, however, is the calculation for a higher rate tax payer.	Yes. A higher rate tax payer gets a lower retirement income than a Basic rate tax payer based on the same contribution level under a property pension, but it's still in excess of the traditional pension.

| 8% Yield | There are many properties and areas that offer an 8% + yield. I have included a list of over 350 areas in the appendix. | Yes. The higher the yield the higher the profit per year, thus reducing your overall contribution. If the yield is 6.75% then the profit over the 25 years matches your contribution to property so that your overall contribution is nil. Below 6.75% yield and you will then have to contribute out of your own pocket. Above 6.75% yield requires no overall contribution. |

Over 75% of properties on the market offer a 6.75% + yield so there is no shortage of suitable properties; 8% + just gives you that comfort margin. Check out the appendix for the 350 areas that offer in excess of 8%.

| Fixed interest rate of 5% APR | A fixed rate had to be used to keep the examples simple. Again we are crystal ball gazing here. 5% APR is reasonable because we can fix interest rates to around this level for a period greater than 10 years. Also, fixed rates are determined by the fixed bond market which is less volatile than the variable rate market. | Yes. The cost of borrowing affects profits quite dramatically if we don't buy at a good yield. If you buy a property in excess of 8% then you can weather interest rate fluctuations. |

You need to consider what you think the average interest rate will be over the next 25 years – and if you know the answer to that then let me know!

| Interest only mortgage taken out | Interest only monthly payments are less than repayment monthly payments, thus monthly cash inflows are higher due to the balance never being reduced. It's a reasonable assumption as all the mortgage companies offer it but it depends on whether you want the property paid in full by the time you hit retirement. | Yes. If the example used a repayment mortgage instead of an interest only mortgage then the profit would be the same but the cashflows would have been different. The monetary difference between repayment and interest only could be considered as a contribution. The beauty is that this contribution can be structured as a voluntary contribution if you took out an interest only mortgage and paid the capital off as and when you wished to. |

Assumption	Reasonable?	Relevant to performance?
Other costs being 20% of rent	20% of rent is quite a generous allowance. This equates to 1 month void period, management fees of 10% of rent and 2% of rent spent on repairs.	Yes. The amounts of voids, management charges and repairs affect profit which affect your overall contribution. You need to consider if 20% is enough.
Professional fees	I have assumed £1,500 for year 5, increasing by £500 every 5 years. This is a standard charge for valuations, solicitor costs and arrangement fees. It's unlikely that you will face a charge greater than £1,500 and the £500 increase every 5 years is above the rate of inflation so is a prudent estimate.	Yes. The size of your contribution is dependent on the amount of professional fees required. The less required means that you can acquire properties sooner as the requirement to purchase a property is lowered.
Deposit level of 15%	There are many 15% deposit level mortgage lenders – and to prove it check out www.moneynet.co.uk	No. 15% is the minimum deposit level required. Since there are many lenders offering 15% deposit level mortgages it's a fair assumption that it's possible to get this type of mortgage.
Property purchase price of £30,000 rising by 5% every year.	I have chosen £30,000 just as a notional figure to compare like with like, based on a rough £100 per month contribution. If a property can only be bought for £90,000 then a contribution of £300 per month is required.	No, as the contributions in both examples were the same. So if £90,000 had to be the purchase price then we would have to alter the contributions in the traditional pension example to £300 per month so we could compare like with like.
5% Growth of property prices	This is a very difficult question as we are crystal ball gazing. We cannot base it on past performance as that is no indication. The key fact is that it is the same growth rate as the traditional pension calculations so neither has an advantage.	No, as both growth rates were set equal.
Start age of 41	The start age is not really relevant as the pensions were being compared.	No. Both start ages were the same.

| Retirement age of 65 | The retirement age is not really relevant as the pensions were being compared. | No. Both retirement ages were the same. |

It's up to you to decide whether these assumptions are reasonable and/or relevant. Try flexing the numbers to see what other results you get. Do whatever it takes for you to come to a decision on whether what I'm saying has some basis or is fundamentally flawed due to very relevant omissions. Until you do this you will always be waivering between traditional pension funds or property pension funds or even something else! *And* always kicking yourself for not making the right decision when one of them booms.

RISKS *v.* RETURNS

So we have established the returns to be had from a traditional pension and a property pension but what are the risks and are they worth it? Lets look at the risks for each one.

The risks involved in investing in property

There are a number of fears that people have which are fully justified. They are not dissimilar to what business people face when appraising a potential investment. These are called risks. The difference between the ordinary person and a business person is that a business person:

(a) Identifies all the risks involved

(b) Mitigates each risk as best he or she can

(c) Considers the overall risk based on how well he or she can mitigate each individual risk

(d) Makes a decision based on the overall risk

So to build a property pension you need to:

(a) Identify all your fears involved in building a property pension

(b) Think how you can overcome each fear involved in building a property pension

(c) Consider the overall fear factor based on how well you can overcome each individual fear

(d) Decide whether you want to build a property pension or not based on the overall fear factor

Fortunately for you I'm not going to ask you to think up all the fears involved, how to overcome these fears and calculate the overall fear factor. I am going to tell you this!

Unfortunately for you I am not going to decide for you whether to build a property pension or not because I am not you! However, I will present a very strong case to you and I will recommend that you build one – but the ultimate decision rests with you.

THE FEARS AND HOW TO OVERCOME THEM

With every fear you can take what I call **Countermeasures** which overcome each fear. A countermeasure is an action you take to counteract each fear. No countermeasure is fool-proof otherwise the fear would not be a fear purely by definition.

There will still always be an overhang of fear albeit a lot less than the initial fear. This is what I call **Residual Fear**. The residual fear is therefore still present even after the countermeasure and thus is a real fear. You can take further countermeasures to reduce this residual fear but it depends on how far you want to go.

There will always be some residual fear, however. An example of a residual fear that cannot be eliminated is the destruction of your property if there were to be a war. No insurance company will take on this risk. The only way you could mitigate this risk would be to build a bomb proof shell around your property – but this would be impractical and probably cost more than your property itself!

The fears, countermeasures and residual fears in buying a property are:

	Fear	Countermeasure	Residual fear	Further countermeasure
1	Can't find a tenant.	Buy a property that can be easily let out, like near a major train station or in a desirable area.	Still can't find a tenant.	Reduce the rent.
2	Interest rate rises beyond affordability.	Fix the interest rate for a fixed period of time.	The interest rate rises beyond affordability after the fixed period of time.	Fix the interest rate for the whole term of the mortgage.
3	Get caught in negative equity trap.	Don't sell the property and realise your loss. Continue to rent it out. Wait for the recovery and then sell.	It never recovers and you have to sell.	Buy the property without a mortgage so that negative equity is not a possibility.
4	The tenant does not pay the rent.	Take out landlord insurance that covers you for loss of rent due to tenant default.	None	N/A
5	Major repair becomes due and can't afford to carry out works.	Take out a thorough and comprehensive buildings and contents insurance.	The policy doesn't capture every eventuality.	Take out specific policies for specific items, e.g. British Gas offer full insurance on your boiler from £8 per month.
6	You buy a property you can't sell.	Avoid difficult to sell properties such as studio flats, ex local authority flats, flats above shops, non-standard construction properties or any property that is difficult to get a mortgage on.	Still can't sell it!	Buy a property near a train station, city or major road junction.

Overall fear

To calculate your overall fear is to gather all the residual fears that remain. To do this you:

(a) Decide which fears listed above 1 to 6 are fears that you actually have

(b) Decide what countermeasures you are willing to take for each fear

(c) Calculate the residual fear for each fear applicable

So, for example, if you had the following fears and were willing to take the following countermeasures, then your overall fear is all the contents of the residual fear column:

	Fear	Countermeasures willing to take	Residual fear
1	Can't find a tenant.	Buy a property that can be easily let out, like near a major train station or in a desirable area and be willing to reduce the rent.	Not being able to find a tenant for a property near a major train station or desirable area even though you are flexible on the rental price.
3	Interest rate rises beyond affordability.	Fix the interest rate for the whole term of the mortgage.	Nil.
4	Get caught in negative equity trap.	Don't sell the property and realise your loss. Continue to rent it out. Wait for the recovery and then sell.	It never recovers and you have to sell.
6	The tenant does not pay the rent.	Take out landlord insurance that covers you for loss of rent due to tenant default.	None.
8	Major repair becomes due and can't afford to carry out works	Take out a thorough and comprehensive buildings and contents insurance as well as specific policies for specific items.	The policies don't capture something you hadn't thought of.

So the overall fear is the total of the residual fear column being:

◆ You do not find a tenant even though you have bought a desirable property and you can reduce the rental price asked.

◆ You buy a property that goes into negative equity and you have to sell.

◆ You get stung for a repair that you never thought you'd get.

You have to make an estimation of how likely these fears are to materialise and whether the rewards from investing in a property pension are compensatory enough. If you can cope with this overall fear then you will invest in property. If you can't then you won't. If you can't cope with the overall fear then I suggest you take more countermeasures so that your overall fear is reduced to a level that you can cope with, so you are comfortable in investing in property.

The risks associated with a traditional pension fund

Because you transfer a lot of your control over to the pension fund manager there are only two real risks:

	Fear	Countermeasure	Residual fear	Further countermeasure
1	The fund is not big enough to pay your desired retirement income.	Contribute more to the fund.	Still isn't big enough.	Wait for annuity rates to rise.
2	At the time of retirement the annuity rates are poor.	Wait for the rates to improve.	Rates do not improve.	Contribute more to the fund.

So in summary you can either add to your fund or wait. These are the only two strategies you have!

SO ARE YOU CONVINCED?

Well, I've laid out both arguments for you but it's for you to come to a decision. Do you think property is better than traditional pension funds? I really want you to study this chapter as this is key to your motivation to build a property pension. Once you are convinced, the motivation to build a property pension will be there. This is because you understand the uniqueness of property and how property is a superior investment to virtually any of the other investments out there.

The illustration above is only one strategy to achieve a property pension. There are many strategies you can adopt to achieve a retirement income but this all depends on YOU. It depends on how much you are willing to contribute, how much you want and when, your attitude to risk and your level of involvement. Let's look at these questions in more detail in the next chapter.

$$\left(2\right)$$

Your Profile

YOUR OBJECTIVE

If you want to build a property pension you need a strategy. A strategy is a method of achieving an objective. So, in this scenario the objective is to:

have an income sufficient enough to meet all your needs in retirement

This is what a pension aims to do but often fails. This is why there are so many charities to help pensioners such as Age Concern and Help The Aged. So to achieve this objective you need a strategy! The first stage in constructing a strategy is to really think about the objective. The objective throws up some obvious questions you need to ask yourself. The obvious questions that need answering, why and how to answer them are:

Question	Why	How To Answer
How much do you need?	You have to know how much you need! If you don't spend the time to think about it then you face the possibility of not having enough. Setting a target income means that you have something to aim for.	On the face of it it seems a difficult question to answer. Your retirement age may be 25 years away and you will have no idea what £1 will be worth in 25 years' time. The fact is you don't need to! What you can do is ask yourself what will you need in today's value of money. Because rental income rises with inflation then all we have to do is express our desired retirement income as rental income at today's value. So if you earn £25,000 per anumn now and would like to keep the lifestyle you have then you require £25,000 rental income at today's rental market value.

Question	Why	How To Answer
		So how much will you need? Think about your likely monthly expenses for living and what you would like to do in your retirement. So don't forget the obvious expenses such as food, bills and clothing and don't forget to omit your mortgage expense if you plan to pay off your home by the time you hit retirement. If you wish to travel in retirement then allow for that expense. So you should be able to come up with a monthly figure.
When do you want it?	You need to know when you wish to retire so you can put a timescale to the objective. You can then set mini-targets within the timescale so you can monitor how well you are doing. If mini-targets are not being met you can adjust your strategy to bring you back on track.	So when do you want to retire? Answering 'tomorrow!' is neither helpful nor practical. Consider your age now, how long you would like to work and what you want to do in your retirement. Remember, retirement can be boring for some people, as many early retirees have admitted. Set a realistic timescale which takes into account your target retirement income.

So an example of someone's objective would be:

Target retirement income at today's value	£25,000
Timescale	18 years

ACHIEVING YOUR OBJECTIVE

Your objective is not going to land in your lap! It requires the following from you:

1. Time
2. Money
3. Acceptance of risk

All these factors are correlated. That is to say if you don't have much money to put in then be prepared to put in more time and accept a higher degree of risk. If you increase the time you put in then you won't have to put so much money in or accept so much risk. Let's look at exactly what's expected from you.

Time

The ways in which your time is needed are shown below, along with ways in which you can reduce that time.

	Time input	Ways to reduce your time input
Acquisition	You need to find the properties that will deliver you an income! This involves researching suitable areas, looking through the local press, speaking to and dealing with agents, visiting prospective properties, arranging finance and whatever else is needed from you to acquire a property.	You can approach a property-buying company that will do all this for you based on your criteria. This costs! These companies can charge up to 5% of the purchase price so they can work out expensive. I offer this service. If you don't have the time and require this service then contact me. My details are in the front of the book.
Find a tenant	You have to advertise, do viewings, credit check and take up references of prospective tenants.	Use a letting agent. They charge a fee of around 10% + VAT on the rent collected.
Legal documents	You need to prepare the legal documents to bound all parties or to evict tenants.	Use a letting agent. They charge a fee of around 10% + VAT on the rent collected. Or use my documents detailed in the Appendix.
Rent collection	You need to arrange for the rent to be collected. This may be face to face collection from the tenant's doorstep, collection from the benefits office or through your bank.	Use a letting agent. They charge a fee of around 10% + VAT on the rent collected. Or you can use my standing order set-up form detailed in the Appendix.
Repairs	You need to either repair the problem or instruct someone to do the repair.	Use a letting agent. They charge a fee of around 10% + VAT on the rent collected.
Tax return	You need to declare what you've earned during the financial year in order to pay tax. This requires accounting for all receipts and expenditure associated with the property.	Use an accountant. Or you can subscribe to www.propertyhotspots.net to manage your finances.

Money

You need money to buy a property! Here is why you need money and ways of minimising the amount needed:

	Needs from you	Ways to reduce the cost
Initial investment	You need a deposit to buy a property. At a minimum it will be 15% of the purchase price. You will also need the associated fees that come with buying a property. These are valuation fees, solicitor costs, arrangement fees, finder fees, initial void period and essential repairs required before letting the property. You need to save for a deposit if you want to buy a property.	You can borrow the deposit and fund the repayments to the loan from the rent achievable once the property has been bought. This increases your risk due the increased borrowing. You can find a property yourself thus eliminating a finder's fee to a property agent. You can buy a property in a good state of repair thus avoiding any essential repair costs.
Monthly contribution	You may have to contribute over and above what is received in rent if you get hit for a large repair bill, interest rates rise, the tenant defaults or you wish to pay off the mortgage early.	Take out insurance on tenant default or any large repairs. This means the insurance company picks up the bill. The cost of this is the insurance premium. Fix your interest rate so fluctuations are not a concern. Thus, if you have chosen a property that returns a rental income in excess of the fixed mortgage payment then you are assured that you do not have to contribute. Take out an interest only mortgage. This keeps the mortgage payment at its lowest possible point so the margin between rent and mortgage cost is at its highest. Go for a higher yielding property. The higher the yield the higher the profit margin. Please note – the higher the yield the higher the risk!

Acceptance of risk

In chapter 1 we dealt with the risks in property. There are always risks in owning an asset but there are also benefits! You can mitigate against these risks at a cost, but there will always be a residual risk remaining. So you will always have to accept a degree of risk.

You need to decide what risks you are willing to take as this will determine the strategies open to you.

YOUR OBLIGATIONS AND YOUR OBJECTIVE

Now these three factors, time, money and acceptance of risk have to bear some relation to your objective.

◆ If your objective is to have a retirement income of £100,000 p.a. at today's value in five years' time and you earn £20,000 p.a., have no savings, no time and are willing to accept only a very low level of risk then it won't happen!

◆ If your objective is to have a retirement income of £100,000 p.a. at today's value in five years' time and you earn £20,000 p.a., have no savings, are willing to contribute a little time and are willing to accept a *high* level of risk then it might happen!

◆ If you wish to earn a retirement income of £20,000 p.a. at today's value in 15 years' time and you earn £20,000 p.a., have no savings but the discipline to save, have a bit of time, and are willing to accept a medium level of risk then it probably will happen.

So how do you know what won't, might or will happen? This is best explained by looking at two extreme scenarios and what's in between.

Target retirement income at today's value	Timescale	Time	Money	Risk	Outcome
Double income being earned today	Less than 5 years	None	No savings and not willing to contribute	Acceptance of low level risk	Won't happen

Target retirement income at today's value	Timescale	Time	Money	Risk	Outcome
Equal or more than income being earned today	Greater than 5 years	Have some time	Have some savings and willing to make ongoing contribution	Acceptance of medium risk	Might happen
Same as income being earned today	Greater than 15 years	Willing to put time in over all aspects	Have savings and willing to make ongoing contribution	Acceptance of medium level of risk	Will happen

So, in my professional opinion, as long as you are willing to earn a retirement income that is what you are earning now, that is 15 years away, have the time, can save and have savings, and accept a medium level of risk then it WILL happen.

BUILDING YOUR PROFILE

Using the information given so far, you should be able to build a profile of yourself and your aims. A profile would be made up of the following:

Profile	Range of answer	Considerations
Target retirement income at today's value	0.5–5 times your actual income now	How much do you want based on today's value? Do you think you will have expensive tastes in retirement? Do you want a simple life in retirement? Or do you just want what you have now?
Timescale	5–30 years	How soon do you want to retire? Is it soon, next decade or next millennium!
Time	Low/Medium/High	Are you willing to be involved in the buying process, rent collection and repairs? Or do you work full-time (and overtime!) and want zero involvement?
Money	Low/Medium/High	Do you have a deposit? Are you good at saving? Are you willing to contribute month by month? Or do you have no savings and require a monthly profit from the properties?

Acceptance of risk	Low/Medium/High	Are you willing to borrow significantly, accept fluctuations in interest rates, take interest only mortgages and go for less desirable properties that yield highly? Or do you want minimal borrowings, fixed rate borrowings, repayment mortgages and nicer properties near your home town?

So a typical profile might be:

Profile	Answer
Target retirement income at today's value	£30,000
Timescale	24 years
Time	Low
Money	Medium
Acceptance of risk	Medium

We can match your profile to the strategies available. What's your profile? Take your time to really think about what you want. Is it realistic? Will it be enough? Do you earn enough to save and/or contribute? Can you take a higher level of risk?

Chapter 3 shows how we can match a strategy, or even a number of strategies, to your profile.

The Three Core Strategies to Building a Property Pension

THE THREE CORE STRATEGIES

There are three core strategies to building a property pension:

1. Buy and then hold

2. Buy and then sell

3. Buy, then part hold and part sell

There are variations within these strategies but every strategy will fall within these core three. Remember from the last chapter the definition of a pension, which we are taking as the objective of a property pension:

have an income sufficient enough to meet all your needs in retirement

Well, the three strategies above can meet this objective.

In more detail:

Strategy	What it entails	Features
Buy and then hold	This involves buying a property (or properties), repaying for it in full by retirement and living off the rental income through retirement.	You rely on the property to be an easily rentable property so as to provide a safe income for retirement.

Buy and then sell	This involves buying a property (or properties), making the repayments during the period of ownership and then selling the property and clearing the debt (if any). The balance of the monies is then used to purchase an annuity to provide an income till death.	You rely on the growth of the property to be sufficient to purchase an annuity to meet your target income in retirement.
Buy, then part hold and part sell	This involves doing a mixture of both strategies above.	Combination of both above.

CHOOSING THE RIGHT STRATEGY

You need to choose the strategy that's right for you based on your level of time, money and acceptance of risk. Here's how these strategies could work with the level of time, money and risk a potential investor has:

Strategy	Level		Refined strategy
Buy and then hold	TIME	Low	Buy a desirable property with less than a 9% yield on a repayment mortgage and place with a letting agent to manage the property. The investor understands that he might have to contribute on top of the rent to cover the mortgage payment but has the assurance that the property will be paid in full. It will then provide an income for life.
	MONEY	Medium	
	RISK	Low	
Buy and then sell	TIME	Medium	Buy a property in a less desirable area but yielding in excess of 10% on an interest only mortgage. The investor will manage the property himself but knows that it is unlikely that he will have to contribute on top of the rent as the property yields high and the mortgage is interest only. He hopes that the property value grows sufficiently in value in order to purchase an annuity to provide him with an income till death.
	MONEY	Low	
	RISK	Medium	

Strategy	Level		Refined strategy
Buy, then part hold and part sell	TIME	High	He does a bit of both above. He is happy to buy more than one property and manage them himself. He uses the profits from some to fund the others but his risk is reduced due to the investor not relying on one single strategy. Overall risk is medium due to the greater exposure he has to the property market but he can capitalise in each market when the market is high.
	MONEY	Medium	
	RISK	Medium	

So think about whether you want to own and run a property or properties pre- and post-retirement. Think about how much money you want to put away for saving up for a deposit and ongoing pre-retirement. Think of the level of risk you want to expose yourself to. Do you want only one property or a few? Do you want repayment or interest only mortgages? Do you require a risk-free income in retirement?

Based on your own profile and personal preferences you should come up with a strategy you want to go for. To help you decide let's look at some examples. I have decided to ignore tax consequences in these examples to keep the figures simple.

Buy and then hold
Richard has the following profile:

Profile	Answer
Target retirement income at today's value	£24,000
Timescale	25 years
Time	Low
Money	Medium
Acceptance of risk	Low

He has decided that he wants to 'buy and then hold' so he can pass the properties down to his children. But he also doesn't want to pass any debt on so he intends to own the property outright. He works full-time so he doesn't want to manage the properties and he wants desirable properties that are easily let out. He has the ability to save and a willingness to contribute on an ongoing basis if need be.

The strategy would to be buy one or more properties that give a rental income of £24,000. As he is a low-risk investor he would buy a low yielding property, such as 8%, on a repayment mortgage. This could be three properties costing £100,000 producing an £8,000 per year income. He will also have the property managed by a letting agent.

I have created a Yield Profit/Contribution Table. This is in Appendix 8. It calculates the profit every month based on a £100,000 purchase price for each yield on an 85% LTV repayment mortgage. The interest rate is set at 5% APR and the term of the mortgage is set as the number of years to retirement. It also allows for 20% of rent to be lost in expenditure and voids.

Property 1
If we look at the Yield Profit/Contribution Table in Appendix 8 for this example we can see that an 8% yield £100,000 value property has a monthly profit figure of £30.75 if the investor is 25 years off retirement. This is how much he would get back every month if he invested from day one. So he knows that if he buys today he will not have to contribute on an ongoing basis and the property will be his in 25 years.

Property 2
The investor knows that he has to buy more than one property if he is to achieve an income of £24,000. Five years later he sees the property next door for sale at £110,000. Because he has been saving he can afford the 15% deposit of £16,500 (being 15% of £110,000). The property is yielding 8% and looking at the table for 8%, with 20 years off retirement, for £100,000 purchase price, the profit is: −£35.05, i.e. £35.05 loss. Because the purchase price is £110,000 then

the loss has to be increased by 1.1 so the overall monthly loss is £38.56.

Property 3

Another five years later the house on the other side is for sale at £120,000 and yielding 8%. He decides to buy again with a 15% deposit of £18,000. So again from the tables, with 15 years to retirement, at 8% yield for £100,000 is £149.09 loss. Multiplying it by 1.2 equals a monthly loss of £178.09

So in summary:

	Deposit	Professional fees	Years off retirement	Monthly profit or loss	Total ongoing contribution
Property 1	−15,000	−1,000	25	35.05	10,515
Property 2	−16,500	−1,500	20	−38.56	−9,254
Property 3	−180,00	−2,000	15	−178.09	−32,056
Total	−49,500	−4,500		−30,795	−84,795

So Richard gets three properties paid in full providing him with a real income of £24,000 per year in 25 years with an overall contribution of £84,795. The likely scenario is that he will contribute nil as the rent will increase with inflation over time to reduce his overall contribution.

If he required an income of £24,000 in real terms from an annuity then his pension fund would have to be £524,246. Based on a pension fund growing by 5% year on year this would mean personal contributions of over £1,000 per month!

Again, play around with the figures to see for yourself that however you tweak the figures a property pension is far superior to a traditional pension. If Richard went for a 9% yield on property 2 and 11% yield for property 3 then his contribution would have been zero.

But because he had a low acceptance of risk he went for the 8% yielding properties all the way.

Please note in this example that, even though Richard owns three properties it doesn't matter what they're worth. Richard owns three properties that we know return £8,000 per year in rental income NOW in 25 years. So it is safe to say that they will provide a real income of £24,000 in 25 years' time. His only risk is if he can't let them or there has been a deflation in rental values.

Using your own home to provide a retirement income

Some people do use their personal home to provide for themselves into retirement. The theory is that you downsize to a smaller property when the kids leave and purchase a bungalow in a quieter area and rent out your own property.

The key things you need to consider are:

- Is the rental value of your home equivalent to your desired income in today's standards?

- Will the property be paid in full when it's time to retire?

- Will you have saved enough to buy a property for yourself to live in?

You can always sell your own home and buy two cheaper properties and live in one and rent out the other. This falls in to the strategy of 'buy and then sell'. But the key things you need to consider above still apply.

Buy and then sell

Susan has the following profile:

Profile	Answer
Target retirement income at today's value	£30,000
Timescale	20 years
Time	Medium
Money	Low
Acceptance of risk	Medium

Susan doesn't earn a lot of money. She earns £15,000 and cannot afford to contribute anything on a monthly basis. But she does have savings of £15,000 left to her by her late grandmother. Susan wants twice her annual income in real terms in her retirement within 20 years! Funnily enough this is possible due to her attitude to risk.

Property 1

She buys a £100,000 property yielding 12% on an interest only mortgage. Looking at the table it provides her with a monthly profit of £445.83. Susan is willing to manage the property herself so we can add at least another £50 per month so let's say her monthly profit is £500 per month.

Property 2

In four years, 48 months, she saves all the profit, being £500 per month, to give her a deposit of £500 × 48 months of £24,000 to buy a property of £160,000 yielding 12%. This gives her another monthly contribution of 1.6 × £500 per month of £800 per month.

Property 3

In two years, 24 months, she saves all the profit, being £1,300 per month, to give her a deposit of £1,300 × 24 months of £31,200 to buy a property of £200,000 yielding 12%. This gives her another monthly contribution of 2 × £500 per month of £1,000 per month.

Property 4

In two years, 24 months, she saves all the profit, being £2,300 per month, to give her a deposit of £2,300 × 24 months of £55,200 to buy a property of £300,000 yielding 12%. This gives her another monthly contribution of 3 × £500 per month of £1,500 per month.

So in summary:

	Deposit	Professional fees	Years off retirement	Monthly profit or loss	Total ongoing contribution	
Property 1	−15,000	−1,000	20	500	120,000	
Property 2	−22,500	−1,500	16	800	153,600	
Property 3	−29,200	−2,000	14	1,000	168,000	
Property 4	−52,700	−2,500	12	1,500	216,000	
Total	**−119,400**	**−7,000**			**657,600**	**531,200**

So overall there is a net profit of £531,200. This goes forward to purchase an annuity. But Susan still owns the properties and their associated debt. The scenario may look like something like this after 20 years from the first purchase:

	Purchase	Value at end of term	Debt	Net value
Property 1	100,000	250,000	85,000	165,000
Property 2	160,000	300,000	137,500	162,500
Property 3	200,000	400,000	170,800	229,200
Property 4	300,000	540,000	247,300	292,700
				849,400

So, if we add up the total value of the fund it gives £531,200 + £849,400 = £1,380,600. At the £45.78 annual income rate per £1000 this would equate to:

£1,380,600 × £45.78/£1,000 = £63,203

This could be the same as £30,000 per year in today's terms or it might not. The fact is that a fund has been amassed with a nil contribution as all the properties (apart from the first purchase) have been funded by the profits from the rent. The beauty is that if the market peaks at any point after Susan has purchased, she is free to sell to maximise her gain. If not she can live off the rental income until it's time to sell.

Now the property purchase prices don't have to be the actual price. So in the above example Susan bought a property worth £300,000. This could have been six properties at £50,000 each (totalling £300,000) being rented out at £6,000 per year. So in fact Susan could end up owning around 20 properties of an average value of £50,000 or so.

Buy, then part hold and part sell

An example of this strategy is to do what both Richard and Susan have done. That is to buy a selection of low, medium and high yielding properties on both interest only and repayment mortgages and allow some properties to fund others.

I would suggest that you choose repayment mortgages for properties that you decide to hold and interest only mortgages for properties you decide to sell.

4

Choosing the *Right* Property in the *Right* Area

So you're convinced that a property pension is better than a traditional pension, you've identified your profile, you've chosen the strategy that suits you best – so where do you buy? This section you'll be relieved to hear is not so number crunching! It's just basic common sense that you will agree with as we all have an intrinsic understanding of property.

CHOOSING THE RIGHT AREA

I have short-listed areas where to invest (in Appendix 3) which give you a yield of 8% or greater. But yield isn't everything! Let me remind you of what a pension actually is:

have an income sufficient enough to meet all your needs in retirement

So *longevity* of rental income is key. The way to establish longevity of rental income is to invest in areas that can provide an income now *and* in the future. These areas have to be desirable to the tenant for whatever reason which keeps tenant demand high. What determines desirability will be the following factors:

Is it an established town or city?

It's quite safe to say that tenant demand will always be high in London. It's our capital city and there will always be an influx of people looking for somewhere to live in London. The problem with London is that the yields are poor. Now if your strategy is to contribute on an ongoing monthly basis then choosing London is not a problem as London will provide a long-term income for life. If you need a higher yield and want quite an assured income then consider other well established towns and cities.

Birmingham is the obvious second choice. But there are others. Look at where major employers are, or are considering moving. Is there a strong infrastructure in place? Follow the news. The Government is considering building all along the M11 corridor. Once the infrastructure is in place the demand for properties there will be high.

Is it a university town or city?

If there is a university in the area then there will always be demand for properties by the students and the employees of the university. If it's a new university then tread carefully. It may not be there in 10 years' time. If it's an old university then you can be assured that it will be there for at least another 40 years.

Is it near a train or tube station?

If your property is next to a tube station in London then people will fight you for your property! You will have no problems letting out your property as not many students have cars and the main way they get about is by tube or bus.

Owning a car is becoming more and more expensive. People are now ditching their cars, saving their money and buying or renting a property closer to a train station. If you're a 10-minute walk to a property from the station then you save on cab fares. Tenants will equate this with cost saving and pay for this luxury.

Is it close to a major road link or airport?

Getting to the main route out of the area can be a nightmare. If you're at the other side of the town from the main junction it can add up to an hour to your journey – especially if you're travelling in rush hour. Having a property next to a main junction (but not on it!) can save people a lot of commuting time. And you know what time equals – money!

Does it have a hospital?

Hospitals employ many people. There will also be many other employers supporting this whole community. The most desirable rental properties are the ones near hospitals. The tenants tend to be good natured compared to others and you get less fuss from them.

Does it have major employers?

If there are large factories or offices littered around the area (that look open!) then this is good news. This means there will be plenty of employed people looking for a rental property. Major employers attract smaller employers and it all filters down.

Does it have a major shopping centre?

If there is a major shopping centre there then it is safe to assume that the residents of this area have money. If they have money then they will be able to pay your rent – well in theory anyway!

People like to shop and the closer the shops are to them the better. So an area is desirable if it has retail parks, large shopping complexes, Tesco Extra etc.

Is there major inward investment into the town or city?

Liverpool has been chosen to be the European City of Culture for 2008. There will be major investment in the city that is expected to change the area for the better. Investors are rushing to buy up everything in sight. Whether Liverpool will change for the better is uncertain to me. But look out for areas that have been ear-marked for inward investment. They could offer you above average capital growth. This will be handy if your strategy is to 'buy and then sell'.

Does it have a good school?

If the area has an established school that appears in the top 10 of the league tables for that area then there will always be demand for properties in that area. Families will pay a rental premium for a property in the catchment area and demand will be high.

Does it have good leisure facilities?

Is there a sports centre or swimming pool in the area? Are there things to do in the area? Does the place have historical interest that attracts visitors? Anything that makes the area a fun place to be or a proud place to live in is a good thing.

Some people have tested the desirability of an area by putting a rogue advert in the local press. They have placed an ad. before they owned any property in that area, for a property at market value rent to see how many calls they got. I have a few properties in Harlow, Essex and I placed an ad. for one of my properties at slightly above market value. I had at least 40 calls and the property was let within two hours of the paper coming out.

Helpful pointers

So you've considered the above and short-listed some areas – what do you look out for? Here are some pointers to help you:

Visit the place!

This may seem obvious but you really have to visit the area a number of times. Consider what impression you get. Is it somewhere you would like to come back to, because you will be if you own property here! Are there tramps or young hooligans hanging around?

Get the local press

Get and *read* the local press. See what's going on. If the front page is about how a guy got murdered last week and pages 2, 3 and 4 all have violent crime reports then the area might not be for you.

Look at developments that the paper is reporting on. Is there a new road being built, a re-opening of a station or a new communal swimming pool being built?

Look for dereliction

Are there any boarded-up properties or shops? Is the high street full of £1 shops and charity shops? Is there wasteland with demolished buildings dotted around the area? If there are signs of neglect then it may be because the council doesn't have the funds to regenerate the area due to lack of residents. But don't jump to conclusions. It could be that there is a new shopping centre being built nearby or the wasteland could be turning into luxury apartments and they haven't been built yet.

Talk to the locals

Strike up a conversation with a local newsagent. Do people like living here or are they thinking of moving out? Do the locals look drab, tired and fed up? Ask about the area and what they know about it. Even if it is chit-chat you'll be surprised at what some locals volunteer.

Get statistics

You can get statistics from the local library (or the internet www.upmystreet.com). Find out crime rates, migration statistics, council tax rates, etc. Whatever you think you need to build a better picture of the area by way of statistics. Remember – you can never have too many statistics!

What are the transport links?

Does the train station have a direct line to London or Gatwick Airport? Does the area connect to a motorway that gets you to a major city within an hour? Connectivity to major hubs is a key factor in providing longevity of income. If it connects well then people will always consider this area within a certain radius.

Is it clean?

The cleanliness of an area can determine the whole feel of the area. Research has shown that it impacts on the behaviour, mood and well being of the residents of the area. Is the area well maintained? Do you get a good feel for the area?

Have the chains moved in?

When you walk down the streets is there a Marks and Spencer, Pizza Express, JD Wetherspoon? If these guys are here then it's likely the residents will stay.

CHOOSING THE RIGHT PROPERTY

So you've decided on an area – what property do you go for? The easy answer to this is a property that appeals to most. The way to achieve this is:

Go for a high demand type

I buy a lot of properties in Stoke-on-Trent. There are rows and rows of 2-bed terraces available to buy and rent but every now and again a 3-bed property comes up for sale. Because there is a shortage of 3-bed + properties they rent very easily. You need to find out what is a high demand type. Due to the conversions of many large properties in London to self-contained flats there is a shortage of 4- and 5-bed homes to rent. These types of properties fly out of a letting agent's window as they are in short supply. Consider number of bedrooms, detached executive properties, fully furnished and more than one bathroom properties.

Fashionable address

If there is a fashionable part of town and people love to live there then consider buying there. You will pay over the odds but if you can go for a low yield then these properties never remain empty for long.

Avoid the unusual

If the property is unusual – perhaps it's a converted windmill, next to a cemetery or made out of timber – then avoid it. You may find tenants but it may take longer than usual. You could find yourself experiencing long void periods between tenancies.

Proximity to facilities

If you go for a property that is near the town centre or local shops, near a school, near a train station or near anything you think is desirable to be near, then you can be assured that it will be desirable to someone.

Proximity to undesirability

Look around the property and see what you can. If the back garden backs on to a rubbish tip or undesirable area then it's best to avoid it. You may find that you get a high turnover of tenants due to them getting fed up with the trouble caused by being near something undesirable.

HELPFUL POINTERS

When viewing a property check for:

Carpets

You have a legal duty to provide floor coverings. If there are no carpets then you will have to pay for new ones.

Kitchen

Is the kitchen big enough to accommodate a small dining table? This is attractive if there is only one reception room and it turns the kitchen into a kitchen–diner.

Smallest bedroom

If the smallest bedroom is smaller than 6ft 6' in any direction then it is not a bedroom! You need to be able to get a bed in a bedroom hence this room can only be considered as a study or a baby's room. You need to take this into account when considering what type of tenant you are looking for. If you are looking for two professional people to share a two-bedroom flat then the second bedroom must be bigger than 6ft 6'.

Bathroom

Is there a fitted shower? A bathroom is a lot more desirable if there is a power shower. If there are two bathrooms then the property is very desirable, even if it is only a shower room.

Heating

Is the heating system old? This can be costly to replace. If possible get it checked prior to purchase. It is your legal duty to provide heating and to issue a gas safety record.

Electrics

Are the electric sockets old? This will tell you that at some point the whole electric system will need rewiring.

Service charges

If it is a flat you will have to pay service charges. Ask the agent if he has any details of the service charges. Some places have exorbitant service charges that render the whole investment unprofitable. Avoid listed buildings as they have frequent redecoration policies that can be expensive.

If the property is in a reasonable condition then buy it. If demand is good there should be no problem letting it out as long as the property is in reasonable condition.

PROPERTY VIEWING RECORD

I have created a Property Viewing Record that can be a useful aide-memoire to have with you when going to look at potential investments:

Property Viewing Record

Estate Agent/Auctioneer

Address of the property

Type of Property

Asking Price

Date of first viewing

Date of second visit

Comments about the Surrounding Area
Schools   Traffic noise   Shops   Public transport   Business units

Outside
Garden and Driveway
Garage
Window Frames/Glass
Walls
Drains/Guttering
Roof

Neighbouring Properties

Inside

Hallway

Lounge

Dining Room

Kitchen

Utility Room

Bedroom 1 (Sizes)

Bedroom 2

Bedroom 3

Bedroom 4

Bathroom

Loft

Potential Work Required

Heating and Plumbing

Electrical Repair

Decoration

Damp Patches

External Lighting

General Observations/Things to Remember

_____

_____

_____

_____

And finally . . .

These are a few little pointers that I have learned that should help you along the way:

◆ Do not believe the myth that a property is only worth buying if you could see yourself living there. The fact is that you aren't going to live there so what is the point of asking yourself if you could live there? You should ask, 'Would *someone* live here?' In a high demand area people will live in a house as long as it has running hot water. I'm sure you've heard the horror stories from people living in London. I knew of 16 Australian and New Zealand backpackers sharing one room! I wouldn't live there, but the landlord found 16 people who would! You have to assess the demand.

◆ Buy the local newspapers and gazettes on the day they advertise local property. If you don't live in the area ask them to send you them on a weekly basis. Telephone all the agents and ask them to recommend the areas which rent the best and the most consistently. Get on the agent's mailing list as a potential investor, and ask for their landlord's pack. This will include details of property they have for rent, and property suitable for a rental investment. This way you can do your homework from one mailing.

◆ Tell the agent you work to strict pricing/bedroom criteria and hold your ground. Most agents will always send you the properties at the top end of your budget because they make more commission this way. Find an agent you can trust to bring you good deals. Watch out for them trying to promote all the one-bed studio flats and maisonettes they can find. This is fine if you are looking at a city with a very fluid population and you are buying in the central district because you want to rent to urban dwelling city workers seeking tiny *pied à terre* properties. Elsewhere, however, think carefully about this type of unit and the difficulties that come with it.

◆ At the other end of the scale don't be tempted into buying one enormous house or a flat with four bedrooms because it may be slow to let and even slower to re-let. Instead consider investing in three two bed flats or two bed terraced properties if that's what the market dictates.

5

Finding the Right Buy-to-Let Mortgage

A buy-to-let mortgage is a relatively new financial product, which emerged onto the market in 1995. It allows anybody to purchase a house or flat with the intention of letting it out. This product allows you to borrow the finance needed to buy the property based on the rental income generated rather than your actual personal income. As long as the rental income is greater than 130% of the interest payment you can purchase the property.

Typically you need 15–25% of the purchase price as a deposit, so for a £100,000 purchase price you need between £15,000 and £25,000 and the lender will fund the other £75,000 to £85,000. A higher deposit is needed relative to a residential property – typically 0–10%, as the property is not owner-occupied and the lender's mortgage payment depends on a suitable and reliable tenant being found. Hence this presents a higher risk to the lender. If they ever had to repossess the property they would only need to achieve 85% of the purchase price. This may only be the true market value of the property after it has been tenanted or if there is a property slump at the time of repossession.

WHAT'S BEST FOR YOU?
The most suitable buy-to-let mortgage for you depends on the following factors:

1. Your deposit level
2. The purchase price

3. The type of property
4. Your personal credit history
5. Your acceptance of risk
6. The degree of aftercare
7. Timescale to retirement
8. Ongoing contribution

Your deposit level

The deposit level (alongside how much you are willing to borrow) dictates the maximum purchase price. This will set out how much you will have to save and for how long. This is best explained in an example:

John earns £25,000 p.a. He can afford to save £200 per month. After five years he has:

60 months $\times$ £200 = £12,000 as a deposit level.

He assumes £1,000 for professional fees and the initial void period, leaving an £11,000 deposit level. Considering that the maximum loan to value is 85% the greatest purchase price is:

£11,000/15% = £73,333

So the maximum he can borrow is £73,333–£11,000 = £62,333. So the following formula holds:

$$\frac{\text{(Initial investment – professional fees)}}{\text{Deposit required in percentage terms}} = \text{maximum purchase price}$$

So if you can buy a property for £73,333 in the area of your choice then your deposit level is sufficient. If there is nothing for sale under £100,000 then you need to save for longer.

It is crucial to calculate the maximum purchase price so you know what you can afford to buy. There is no point looking at a property that is in excess of this maximum as no lender will lend in excess of 85% Loan to Value (LTV). If you can't find what you want then you're going to have to save some more! So the deposit level is key to the whole thing – you need to have enough.

It is also important to ensure your maximum purchase price is in excess of the lender's minimum purchase price – see below.

The purchase price

Almost all lenders have a minimum purchase price. The minimum purchase price starts at £6,500 and rises to £75,000 for certain lenders. If *your* purchase price is below *their* minimum purchase price then the lender will not consider you under any circumstances. So the purchase price can dictate the mortgage you can get.

The type of property

Lenders have certain exclusions based on the type of property. The key exclusions are:

1. **Studio flats** – These are flats that have one main room that is used as a lounge and bedroom, plus a kitchen and a bathroom. They are excluded, as they could be difficult to sell if there was a property price slump.

2. **Ex-local authority houses and flats** – These are properties that were once owned by the local council and subsequently sold on to private people. They are excluded, as they are associated with the lower end of the property market.

3. **Flats above commercial properties** – These are excluded as the commercial property below could be let out to a fast food take-away business at some later date. The smell of the food would lead to a decline in the market value of the property.

4. **Flats with more than four storeys in the block** – These are considered as a high-rise block and at the lower end of the property market.

5. **Multiple-title properties** – These are properties where a freehold exists with a number of long leases and you are trying to buy the freehold. An example of this is a block of flats.

6. **Non-standard construction** – If a house is not built with bricks or does not have a pitched tile roof it is deemed non-standard. For example, some houses may be constructed from poured concrete. Despite being perfectly fine houses, lenders may consider these properties inferior to the standard construction properties.

The type of property can dictate the mortgage you can get.

Your personal credit history

What the lender is trying to establish is – are you a good bet? They will need to know that they will get back their money plus interest with the minimum of effort. They will need to establish whether you are creditworthy.

There are two main credit reference agencies that all lenders consult before they make any lending decision, Experian and Equifax. They record a number of details about you based on your current and previous addresses in the last three years, namely:

1. **Electoral roll** – Details of whether you are on the electoral roll as some lenders require you to be on it before they can lend.

2. **County Court Judgments (CCJs)** – These arise when a debtor has taken you to court to enforce payment of a debt and the debtor won the case. The court holds this information for six years from the date of the judgment. They also record if you subsequently paid the judgement.

3. **Individual Voluntary Arrangements (IVAs)** – This is where you have become bankrupt and unable to pay your debts. Once you have been made bankrupt and the debts have been settled then you become a discharged bankrupt. Only once you have been dis-

charged can you have any hope of obtaining credit again. You are automatically discharged after six years.

4. **Credit accounts** – These are all your loan accounts that have been active in the last six years and whether you have ever defaulted on them. Typical accounts are your mortgage account, credit and store card accounts and personal loans.

5. **Repossessions** – Details of any house repossessions that have ever occurred.

6. **Previous searches** – These are previous credit searches by other lenders that you have made a credit application with.

7. **Gone Away Information Network (GAIN)** – This is where you have moved home and not forwarded the new address and not satisfied the debt.

8. **Credit Industry Fraud Avoidance System (CIFAS)** – This is where the lender suspects fraud and just flags it up. You cannot be refused credit based on a suspicion.

Your credit file dictates the mortgage you can get. The key factors are CCJs or defaults. If you have any CCJs or defaults (points 2 and 4 above) you will be restricted to adverse credit lenders who charge higher arrangement fees and interest rates. If you have an IVA, repossession or GAIN on your file it is unlikely you will get a buy-to-let mortgage but you will still probably be able to get a residential mortgage, depending on when you had debt problems. It is worth noting that the buy-to-let mortgage market is further developing and a suitable product may come on to the market soon.

There is one key thing you should remember when filling out your form – do not lie! If lenders find out they will demand repayment in full and they could inform the police of fraud – the charge being obtaining finance by deception. The credit reference agencies are becoming more and more sophisticated. They log every bit of information you put on every credit application and if you submit an application that was slightly different from a previous application they will flag it up.

Your acceptance of risk

As discussed earlier, your acceptance of risk is key to the level of exposure you want to have over events that are out of your control. When it comes to mortgages the only real risk is the interest rate. There are only two categories of type of interest rate – fixed or variable. There are various sub-categories of these in the table below:

Type	Narrative
FIXED	
Fixed	This is for the low risk-taker. It ensures that the monthly mortgage payment is fixed for a period of time, usually between 1 and 10 years.
Capped	This is also for a low risk-taker. It ensures that the mortgage payment never exceeds a certain amount but if interest rates fall then your mortgage payment can fall. No downside risk and only upside potential!
VARIABLE	
Tracker	This is where the interest rate being charged follows the exact rate being set by the Bank of England + a buy-to-let interest loading, typically 1–2%. You are fully exposed to the Bank of England interest rate fluctuations.
Discount	This is where the initial interest rate is discounted by 1–4% for a specified period of time. This could be a discount on a tracker or a standard variable rate. You are exposed, but because there is a discount in place you don't feel the fluctuations quite as badly.
Stepped	This is where the discount is reduced over a number of years. So you would be entitled to a 3% discount in year 1, 2% discount in year 2 and 1% discount in year 3 for example.
Variable	This is just the standard variable rate set by the lender. Your mortgage payments are fully exposed to interest rate fluctuations.

You have to be careful of the tie-in/lock-in periods that may exist with all these products. These are the minimum periods that you have to remain with the lender without incurring financial penalties if you wish to redeem the loan because you want to sell or remortgage the property.

Some lenders provide all the mortgages above and some lenders only provide some of these mortgages. The type of mortgage you want dictates the lender you have to approach.

The degree of aftercare

Some people require face-to-face contact with their lender. If this is so, then you can really only approach high street banks and building societies. There are many lenders who do not talk to the public and only liaise with your mortgage broker. Personally I don't mind not having face-to-face contact, as my mortgage broker is quite efficient in handling my queries.

Timescale to retirement

The duration of the mortgage needs to fit in with your strategy of when you wish to retire. If you wish the duration of the repayment mortgage to be 30 years and the maximum term being offered by one lender is 25 years then this lender is not usable. You need to source the lender that meets your own timescales.

Ongoing contribution

If you need to earn a positive cashflow from your property investment and this is only possible from an interest-only mortgage or a long-term repayment mortgage then you can only apply to interest-only mortgage lenders or lenders that have a longer than usual term.

TYPICAL PROFILE

So after considering the seven factors dictating the type of mortgage you can get, you can build a profile that looks like this:

Factor	Profile
Maximum purchase price	£80,000
The purchase price	£75,000
The type of property	Private one-bedroom flat standard construction
Your personal credit history	Clean
Fixed or variable?	Fixed capped (no lock-in period)

Factor	Profile
The degree of aftercare	High street bank or building society
Timescale to retirement	24 years and interest only
Ongoing contribution	Nil

With this profile you can approach a mortgage broker and he/she will be able to source a lender that meets your profile. I would advise that you make an application with a lender before you find the property so that when you do find a property you can act quickly if need be.

MORTGAGE BROKERS

A local mortgage broker can be found quite easily through the yellow pages or www.yell.com. You can use my mortgage broker if you wish. Her name is Liz Syms and she can be contacted on Tel: 01708 443334, Fax: 01708 470043. If you mention the reference 'Ajay Ahuja', you will receive a discount. She is very good – this is why I use her! If not, I suggest you still go for a buy-to-let specialist mortgage broker.

6

Finding the Right Tenant

It's no good just finding a tenant. It has to be the *right* tenant. The right tenant will depend on the following factors:

1. The property
2. You!
3. Your lender

THE PROPERTY

If you have acquired a private one-bedroom riverside apartment in a central location, then a single parent on benefits is probably not the most suitable tenant. When looking at properties it's a good idea to build up a picture of the tenant you think is most suited to it. A tenant can only fall into one of eight general categories based on the size of the family unit and whether they are working or claiming benefit. The table below suggests which property is suited to each category of tenant:

	Claiming benefit	Working
Single person	Ex-local authority studio or one-bedroom flat.	Any – he/she may require just a room to lay his/her head or a three-bedroom house because he/she wants a computer room and a spare room. If he/she can pay the rent, then he/she can dictate where he/she wants to live.
Single parent	Two-bedroom + ex-local authority flat. If you let a one-bedroom flat to them they will only be looking to move to somewhere bigger and you will have to find another tenant.	Two-bedroom ex-local authority or private house is preferable, as it will have a garden.

	Claiming benefit	Working
Couple	Ex-local authority studio/one-bedroom flat only. DSS are unlikely to pay market rent for a two-bedroom flat for a couple when they can quite comfortably live in a studio/one-bedroom flat.	Any – for the same reasons as above.
Family	Two-bedroom + ex-local authority house. A family will invariably want a property with a garden.	Two-bedroom + ex-local authority or private house. A family will invariably want a property with a garden.

So, if you buy a private one-bedroom flat you know that the right tenant is a working single person or couple. You need only advertise for that tenant – 'suit working person or couple', the advert might read. If you misplace a tenant at your property it will only lead to the hassle of finding another tenant later on. It's worth noting that a two-bedroom + ex-local authority house meets six out of the eight tenant categories.

You could use this table to dictate the type of property you buy. For example, if there are a lot of single parent DSS claimants in the area looking for properties then a two-bedroom ex-local authority flat might be the right property to go for. If you wish to go for the minimum risk route then go for the two-bedroom + ex-local authority house.

YOU!

If you are going to manage the property yourself then the most important person in this whole tenant-choosing process is YOU! If you feel you can get on and deal with only a certain category of people then choose them exclusively. If you're a professional person used to dealing with only professional people then steer towards private properties in the nicer areas.

Personally I have no reservations or hang ups – apart from two:

1. People who can't speak English
2. Young couples under 25

It can be very difficult to extract rent from tenants when you cannot communicate with them. If there is an initial language barrier then I can only foresee problems, unless there is an intermediary, like a social services officer because social services are paying the rent. Otherwise steer clear of such tenants.

Couples aged under 25 can sometimes be troublesome. The tenancy will only last as long as the relationship does. They think it's a great idea to move in together after knowing each other for only two months, but if/when the couple fall out, neither one takes responsibility for the rent, you're left with the task of chasing them both independently for the rent and if they each blame the other, you're the loser. If a couple under 25 are the only ones interested in the property ask them how long they have been together and if they have lived together before. Try to get a larger deposit – two months is ideal. Also try to get one of their parents to be a guarantor.

YOUR LENDER

If you are borrowing to finance the property purchase then lenders often stipulate what type of tenant you can have. The main exclusions are DSS claimants and student lets. You need to check with your lender what exclusions they have and let this be the criteria for your selection of the lender.

ADVERTISING FOR A TENANT

There are five main ways of advertising for a tenant. Let us consider the cheapest form of advertising first:

1. Contacting the local council
2. Advertising with large local employers   FREE
3. Contacting accommodation projects
4. Advertising in the local press
5. Through a letting agent

Contacting the local council

Councils have a waiting list of people looking for a place to live. Since councils have fewer council properties on their books, they are always pleased to hear from private landlords willing to let their properties to residents in the local area. The councils have lists of working and unemployed people as well as refugees and asylum seekers.

I would advise that you write a letter detailing the property you have to let to the Housing Section of the local council and follow it up with a phone call. Councils can be slow so I would not rely on this as your only source of finding a tenant.

Advertising with large local employers

There are two large local employers in the Harlow area. I wrote to both of their human resources departments detailing that I had various properties for their employees. I get a call once every other month, so I would not rely on this as your only source of finding a tenant.

Contacting local accommodation projects

Local accommodation projects are always on the lookout for willing landlords to take on 'homeless' people in the area. The 'homeless' does not mean that they are currently living rough – they simply do not have a fixed place of accommodation. These projects usually collect the rent and guarantee the rent if the tenant fails to pay. They do not charge for their services, as they are charities or non-profit organisations.

Advertising in the local press

This is probably the most effective way of advertising. It is best to advertise in a paper that is delivered free locally so that your advert reaches every resident in that area. There are certain key elements you need to put in your advert:

◆ **Area** – You must say where the property is. It is no good assuming that the reader will know the area where the property is when the newspaper is distributed in a number of local areas. This way you avoid unwanted calls.

- **Private** – If it is in a private area that is a selling point.

- **Furnished** – Again, if it is furnished say so.

- **Number of bedrooms** – You must put the number of bedrooms the property has as readers will then know if your property can accommodate them.

- **Price** – In any advert you must put the price. I always quote my properties as weekly rent e.g. £80 per week. This way the tenant assumes that the rent is £320 per month (as the tenant thinks there are four weeks in a month when there are actually 4.33 weeks in a month) when in fact it is £346 per *calendar* month. Your property will appear cheaper than other properties that are quoted per calendar month. If you price your property at £79 rather than £80 the impact is even more significant.

- **Features** – If it's got a new bathroom then say so! Anything that is not standard with a property such as a garage, separate dining room, large garden or new carpets will attract more interest.

- **Telephone number** – Do not give out your mobile number only! You will receive fewer calls as everyone knows that a five-minute call to a mobile costs a small fortune, especially to the people who you are trying to target. Put a landline down as well as a mobile. I have a freephone number which costs me 4p per minute to receive – a small price to pay to get someone talking about your property. Freephone providers are detailed in the reference chapter.

To find out about the local newspaper in the area of the property you have bought or are thinking about buying, visit www.newspapersoc. org.uk.

Finding a tenant through a letting agent

This is the most expensive way to find a tenant. They usually charge one month's rent + VAT. But they will show prospective tenants round, run credit checks, ask for references, arrange a standing order and do an inventory check on the property. I would recommend this if you work or live far away from the property.

IF YOU CAN'T LET THE PROPERTY

If you are having trouble letting the property, there are a number of things you can do. I suggest you do these in time order:

Reduce the rent

If you can't let it out at the price you want, then reduce the rent. It's the basic economics of supply and demand. I suggest reducing the rent by £2 per week increments.

Widen the criteria for the type of tenant wanted

If you've asked for non-smokers then consider smokers. The smell can be eradicated quite easily by a local cleaning company if need be.

Accept a tenant without a deposit

A letting agent would be horrified by this advice. However, I have done this on a number of occasions, especially for DSS claimants who simply do not have that kind of cash to pay. I recommend this approach for properties that are not in the best of condition, and where the tenant is a family on benefits so the claim will go through smoothly. You have to ask yourself whether the tenant can do any more damage to the property considering its current state. Most people are looking for a place they can call home rather than moving into somewhere with the intention of wrecking it three months down the line.

Furnish the property

This will be expensive and is no guarantee that the place will attract tenants. Consider this if you are getting calls rejecting the property because it is unfurnished.

Sell it!

This is a drastic measure as I think any property in the UK is lettable – it's simply the rent you are asking for that will deter possible tenants. However, if you are experiencing trouble letting it, get out! Sell it and buy something else.

CREDIT CHECKING YOUR TENANTS

You can check the credit of your tenant like a lender credit checks a borrower. This costs between £17.50 and £94.00, depending on what service you require. Some credit checking agencies guarantee the rent if your tenant defaults. All letting agents insist that landlords do this but I disagree. Credit checks are advisable for only certain types of tenants and areas. Let me explain by way of a table detailing the different types of tenant (private or DSS) and area (low and high demand for rental properties). A yes in the box means you should credit check your tenant.

		TENANT	
		Private	Benefit claimant
AREA	High demand for rental property	Yes	No
	Low demand for rental property	No	No

So only in one out of four circumstances would you normally obtain a credit check on your prospective tenant? The justification for this is as follows:

◆ **Private tenant in high demand area** – As the tenant is paying all the rent and you can afford to be choosy as there is high demand for your property, then it is worth credit checking. This ensures that you get the best tenant. I would strongly advise you to get an employer's reference as well, confirming that the company employs him/her, and use the credit check as only a supporting tool.

◆ **Private tenant in low demand area** – If you have had few calls for your property and you wish to only have a private tenant then you cannot be choosy. Most people will fail a credit check – even I do. I am a chartered accountant but I have a default that I am currently investigating from 18 months ago for £4.89, which renders my credit check as a failure. So a credit check does not always guarantee the best tenant but can only support the tenant's case. That's why it's important to get an employer's reference.

◆ **DSS tenant in high demand area** – The council pays the majority of the rent so there is no point credit checking a tenant for, say, a £10 a week top-up. The tenant would probably fail the check anyway.

◆ **DSS tenant in low demand area** – The same reason as above.

Credit checking is also dependent on your acceptance of risk. If you have a low acceptance of risk then it is probably advisable to get the full credit check that guarantees the rent if the tenant fails. If you are willing to accept some degree of risk then it is advisable to get a credit check in the circumstances noted above. If you are a risk taker like me then never get a credit check. Get an employer's reference.

I use my common sense and intuition – it hasn't failed me yet. A prospective tenant who fails a credit check could be better than a tenant who passes a credit check. Let me explain. The two most common causes for someone failing a credit check even though their credit rating is still good are:

1. **They've never had credit** – Just because someone has never had credit does not make them uncreditworthy. For example, you may have a university graduate looking to move into your property as they have just got their first job in the area. They may be from a good family who will bail them out if they get into any money problems. One would imagine that they are responsible enough to take the financial commitment of a tenancy considering they have gone to university. They will probably be earning in excess of the national average wage and will be able to comfortably afford the rent. Taking these factors on board they may still fail a credit check. However, they may be the most suitable tenant for your property after taking *everything* into consideration.

2. **Low value defaults** – I have a default for £4.89 from 18 months ago which I am currently investigating. I would fail some credit checks

because of this. A £4.89 default does not make me uncreditworthy under any circumstances. You have to look at the tenant's situation as a whole rather than whether he passes or fails a credit check. Do not be afraid to ask what they earn and compare that to the rent you are charging. If the monthly rent is approximately a third of their monthly income then they can probably afford it.

The most common causes for a tenant to pass a credit check but ultimately end up defaulting are:

1. **They lose their job** – No amount of credit checking can predict this.

2. **The tenant household splits up** – When couples split up, their financial commitments are the last to get a look-in. If you've let to a group of students and one of them leaves it can then be very difficult to chase him or her or to get the rest of the household to make up the difference. Just because a tenant passes a credit check now does not mean that they will honour their commitments in the future. Their circumstances may change – this is why people default!

3. **The tenant misbudgeted** – If this is the first time the tenant has ever taken on the responsibility of occupying and paying for a home then it is possible that the tenant has miscalculated or omitted some of the other costs associated with running a home. Add in rates, council tax, electricity, etc. and the tenant quickly falls in arrears. Ask the tenant if they have ever run their own household and ascertain if the tenant is aware of all the costs involved in doing so.

So you can see that credit checks have limited use. The key questions you need to be asking yourself about the prospective tenant are:

◆ Can they afford the rent now and in the future?

◆ Have they got a temporary or permanent job?

- Have they got a supportive family and can you get them to be guarantors for the rent?

- Do they appear to know all the costs involved in running a household?

I assume that if someone can afford to pay over a month's deposit and one week's rent in advance then he or she will probably be able to pay the rent in the future. So far I have not been wrong. The times I have been wrong is when I have not taken a deposit and let a tenant move in with just one week's rent in advance. The tenant quickly falls into arrears because they cannot budget. That is why they never had a deposit in the first place!

DEALING WITH COUNCILS FOR HOUSING BENEFIT PAYMENTS (DSS)

If you decide to accept someone on benefits, then the local council will pay most of the rent. Many investors do not like DSS tenants but I have had little trouble with this type of tenant, and once set up, the rent simply arrives on your doorstep. There are a number of key factors when dealing with the DSS:

- **You will get paid four weeks in arrears** – All councils pay four weeks in *arrears*. If cashflow is crucial then do not take on DSS tenants. Invariably the council payment will take anywhere between four weeks and sixteen weeks to get paid. This is because you depend on the tenant providing all the information the council requires. If the tenant is slow to respond to the council consider issuing notices of eviction to the tenant to hurry him/her up.

- **Ensure that the benefit cheques get paid direct to you** – All housing benefit can be paid directly to the landlord if the tenant signs a consent form. This is a must if you take on DSS tenants. This way you get paid directly by the council, rather than by the tenant, who may be juggling his/her income and may find paying rent is not a priority.

◆ **Clawbacks** – Be aware that if your tenant has been fraudulently claiming benefit then the council can reclaim all the housing benefit that has been paid to you. I've heard some horror stories where clawbacks have totalled £2,500! If you are risk-averse, stick to private tenants.

THE LANDLORD–TENANT RELATIONSHIP

Your tenant is not your friend! If your friend approaches you wishing to live in one of your properties then say no – make some excuse. We all know the feeling when we've lent a friend £20 on a night out and then we have to ask for the money back – we all hate doing it. There is a good reason why we don't like doing so and that is because money and friends don't mix. Many friends in the past have fallen out over very small amounts of money, let alone a month's rent.

If your tenant tries to become friendly with you, like inviting you to their Christmas party, always decline. The relationship between landlord and tenant is strictly a business relationship and if this becomes blurred, then you are heading for trouble. This does not mean you have to be overly distant. Remember that you are in business with each other and that is the only reason why you know each other. For the relationship to last, the following simple contract needs to hold – you are supplying a safe property for the tenant to live in and the tenant is paying you the rent on time. Do not complicate matters by drifting into a friendship/business relationship.

COLLECTING YOUR RENT

You can collect your rent in four main ways:

1. Using a letting agent
2. Via your bank
3. Through the post
4. Face-to-face

Apart from using a letting agent, *the way to collect the rent should be dictated by the tenant*. You need to make the way the tenant pays their rent as easy as possible and this will be determined by the tenant. Your choice of tenant should not be dictated by the ease of collection of rent. The choice of tenant should be dictated by the factors mentioned above. It is your duty to work around the tenant if you want the right tenant and to receive the rent on time.

Using a letting agent

Letting agents can handle the whole process of letting your property. This involves finding a tenant, taking inventories, collecting or guaranteeing rent and dealing with all tenant and property problems – sounds too good to be true. However, letting agents are expensive! For a full management service the fee charged can range from 12% to 20% + VAT of the *rent* collected. We accountants call this 'top line commission'. It is called this because they are charging commission on the rental income rather than the overall profit you are making. The expression 'top line' comes from the fact that income is the top line in any profit or loss account.

An agent's fee can wipe out a significant proportion of the profit you potentially could make. Look at this following example, where method 1 is with an agent and method 2 is without an agent:

	Method 1	Method 2
Rental income	400	400
Mortgage	(200)	(200)
Building insurance	(10)	(10)
Sundry expenses	(10)	(10)
Agent's fee (15% + VAT)	(70)	Nil
Net profit	110	180

We can see that a 15% agent's fee can reduce your net profit by 40% – basically just under halving the profit you would make if you did not have an agent! That is not to say you should not use an agent. You need to decide how involved you wish to be in the day-to-day running of the property you have just bought. I would use an agent in the following circumstances:

1. **You work full-time** – This is not to say that you shouldn't try without the help of an agent. I have a few properties that I have never seen since I first let them or I haven't spoken to the tenant since I first met them. This is because the tenant's rent is paid directly into my bank account by standing order and nothing has gone wrong with the flat since I bought it. In this situation, who needs an agent? Only use an agent once letting your property has eaten into your leisure time or you've just simply got fed up. You do not need your tenant ringing you up complaining of a blocked drain when you are in the middle of an important meeting!

2. **The property is far away** – If a property is more than three hours' travel time away then it is probably better to use an agent. The gross yield must be very good though. I would say 24% is the minimum if not higher. This is because you are using an agent and if you were only receiving a 12% yield, after agent fees you would be making a loss.

When I first started I used an agent as I worked full-time and did not want to get bothered at work when something went wrong. Sometimes it can be very time-consuming chasing your tenant for rent. Remember letting agents are experts in handling tenants and cannot only do what you do, they can do it better – that's their business!

I would advise you to use an Association of Residential Letting Agents (ARLA) accredited agent as you are then insured against frauds committed by the agent and bankruptcy of the agent. This means that you would receive all the rents collected by the agent even if the rents were not handed over by the agent. Proof of the fraud would not be needed as the rents are covered by an insurance scheme backed by ARLA.

ARLA agents can be found by visiting www.arla.co.uk.

Via your bank

Assuming your tenant has a bank account then you can set up a standing order which deposits the rent directly into your bank account from the tenant's bank account. I suggest you use the template in the Appendix 7 and ensure that it is sent to the tenant's bank branch at the time of the tenant signing the lease. This template will set up the standing order.

Another way you can collect rent through your bank is to ask the tenant to give you a series of post-dated cheques to cover the rent. So, for example, if he is to pay a rent of £400 on the first day of the month then ask for six cheques for £400 dated the first of the month for the next six months. You then simply present these cheques when the cheque dates become valid.

You could also give your tenant a paying-in book for your bank account. This is best for tenants who earn cash but do not have a bank account. This way the tenant could visit your branch and deposit the rent when possible rather than you both organising a rendezvous for the tenant to hand over the cash.

Through the post
I receive the majority of my rent through the post. This is either from the tenants themselves or from the council housing benefit departments. I prefer this method as it is easier to keep a mental check of who is supposed to be paying (because a cheque physically lands at your door on a regular basis), rather than continuously checking your bank account.

I have one tenant who consistently sends me the rent cheque by recorded delivery. As I am never up when the postman knocks on my door (around 8 a.m.) I have to go to the sorting office to get my cheque. I asked my tenant not to send it by recorded delivery but he prefers to do it that way so I have to accept that I have to go to the sorting office every week! Remember, the tenant always dictates the method of payment.

Under no circumstances should you allow the tenant to pay cash through the post.

Face-to-face

It is unlikely that the tenant will insist on face-to-face collection of the rent. You may feel more comfortable collecting the rent face-to-face so you can see what state the property is being kept in. If the tenant is happy with you collecting the rent that way, it is important that you do not let them feel that you are checking up on them. This will make them feel uncomfortable and could lead to them moving out. If you have chosen your tenant right you will not need to check up on them so often and you can revert to the payment method that suits the tenant.

$$\bigodot 7$$

Paying Tax

We all hate paying tax – but we have to. This chapter deals with the key figures when calculating your tax and how to legally minimise your tax bill. Let's identify the types of tax you will be subject to if you invest in property.

TYPES OF TAX

There are two types of tax that property is subject to:

1. **Income Tax** – This tax is applied to the profit generated from the renting out of the property. It has to be paid every year in half-yearly instalments on 31st January and 31st July. Taxable profit is deemed to be:

   Taxable rental income − allowable expenditure = taxable profit

   Taxable rental income and more importantly, allowable expenditure will be defined in detail so you can easily calculate and *reduce* your taxable profit by claiming all allowable expenditure.

2. **Capital Gains Tax** – This tax is only applied once the property has been sold. It is essentially the tax applied to the profit you have made from selling the property.

Detailed below are certain reliefs that you can claim to minimise your capital gains tax bill to zero!

Income tax

You will only ever pay tax on your taxable profits, that is to say you have to make money before you pay tax. Income has to exceed expenditure – if you have not achieved this then you should not even be interested in this chapter. If you are in the position where income does exceed expenditure then read on.

The equation

The simple equation for calculating your income tax bill is:

Taxable rental income – allowable expenditure = taxable profit

So in order for your taxable profit to be the lowest possible then the 'taxable rental income' must be *minimised* and the 'allowable expenditure' must be *maximised*.

Minimising 'taxable rental income'

This is very difficult to do. Taxable rental income is deemed to be any rental income earned in the period, the period usually being the tax year 6th April XX to 5th April XY. 'Earned' means not only what the tenant has paid but also what the tenant owes even if it has not been paid yet. Basically there are no tricks in reducing taxable rental income, apart from one – if a tenant is 14 days in arrears then you can consider that debt as a bad debt and not include this as taxable rental income. The reason you can do this is because you can file for eviction of your tenant if they fall 14 days behind. If the tenant does end up paying, then you can include the income in the following accounting period. Fourteen days' outstanding rent is in real terms not that much and you'll have to pay tax on the income in the following year anyway. The only real benefit is cashflow. This is because you save slightly on your tax bill and defer payment on this omitted rental income until your next tax return the following year.

Maximising 'allowable expenditure'

This is easier to do than minimising rental income. This is because the Inland Revenue grants certain allowances based on certain definitions as well as allowable expenditure. This means expenditure and allowances can be deducted from the taxable rental income to derive the taxable profit. The two pure definitions that you need to remember for allowable expenditure and taxable allowances, as stated by the Inland Revenue, are:

1. 'Any costs you incur for the sole purposes of earning business profits'

2. 'Capital allowances on the cost of buying a capital asset, or a wear and tear allowance for furnished lettings'

Costs incurred for the sole purposes of earning business profits

Any expense you incur 'wholly, necessarily and exclusively' for the business is *fully* deductible from your rental income. Any personal expenditure that you make that relates to the business is *partly* tax deductible from your income. To make sure you include all expenses that are allowable against your rental income refer to this checklist of expenses for inclusion in your tax return:

Fully tax deductible expenses

Repairs and maintenance

All repairs and maintenance costs are fully tax deductible. Where the property has been altered extensively so as to deem the property being reconstructed, the property is then considered to be modified rather than repaired, hence no amount of the expense is allowed. The only amount allowed would be the estimated cost of maintenance or repair made unnecessary by the modification. Examples of repairs and maintenance expenditure that are fully tax deductible are:

- Painting and decoration
- Damp treatment
- Roof repairs
- Repairs to goods supplied with the property, e.g. washing machine

Finance charges

Any interest you pay on a loan that you took out to acquire a property is fully tax deductible. It is only the interest and not the capital repayment part that is tax deductible. If any of the finance raised (the loan) is used for personal use, such as a holiday, then the interest paid on the amount paid for the holiday is not tax deductible.

The typical interest payments that are allowed are:

♦ Interest on the mortgage taken out to get the property

♦ Interest on any secured or unsecured loans taken out to get the property

Arrangement fees charged by a lender are also tax deductible.

Interest paid on the car you use to run the property business is partly tax deductible – see below.

Legal and professional fees

Allowable expenditures are:

♦ Letting agent's fees for the collection in rent including the VAT (unless you are VAT registered)

♦ Legal fees for evicting tenants

♦ Accountancy fees for preparing your accounts

Disallowable expenditure is:

♦ Surveyor fees initially paid out to value the property (unless the survey was unsuccessful and you never acquired the property, in which case it is a fully deductible expense)

♦ Legal fees incurred due to the purchase of the property

These expenses are added to the purchase price. When it comes to calculating the capital gain when you sell the property:

Gain = selling price − purchase price

This results in the purchase price being higher than the actual price paid due to the addition of initial professional fees. So the taxable gain is lower. These fees are subject to full indexation, as is the purchase price, to allow for price inflation – see Capital Gains section below. So you do get some tax relief but only further down the line, when you sell the property.

Council tax, electricity, water and gas

If you are renting out all the rooms then all the usual running costs involved with a property are fully tax deductible. This assumes that none of the tenants makes a contribution to the bills. If you let out your property inclusive of all the bills then you can fully charge all the bills you include with the rent. If you let out your property exclusive of all bills (which is the usual way) then you cannot claim. Remember, you can only claim the expense if you actually paid it!

Insurances

◆ Buildings insurance
◆ Contents insurance
◆ Rental guarantee insurance

are fully tax deductible. Life assurance premiums are not as this is personal expenditure. Car insurance is, but only partly – see below.

Advertising

Any advertising costs in connection with finding a tenant or selling your property are fully tax deductible. This includes:

◆ Newspaper adverts
◆ Agent's commission

Ground rent

This is the rent you pay if you own a leasehold flat, typically a nominal amount of £50 per annum.

Service charges

Service charges are incurred if you own a leasehold flat. If you pay these charges then they are fully tax deductible.

Letting agent fees

Any fee that is charged by a letting agent is fully tax deductible, apart from any fees charged for leases created for longer than a year. If a fee is charged for creating a 5-year lease then only one fifth of the fee can be charged for each year.

Stationery

Any stationery costs incurred in connection with running your property business are fully tax deductible. This will include items such as:

◆ All paper and envelopes
◆ Postage
◆ All printing expenditure

Partly tax deductible expenses

Motor expenses

Motor costs are allowable but only when your car is used in connection with the property business. It is up to you to decide how much time you think you spend using your car for private use and business use. It has to be reasonable. Once you have decided on the split of personal to business, say 70% personal, 30% business, then you can charge the business percentage against your taxable rental income, in this case 30%. Typical motor expenses are:

◆ Car insurance
◆ Petrol
◆ Servicing and repairs
◆ Interest paid on the loan taken out to acquire the car

A fraction of the purchase price of the car can also be taken into account as an allowance – see below.

I charge 80% of my motor expenses to the business. This is because I have 43 properties to maintain around the country and I spend 80% of my driving time on business engagements.

Telephone calls

Again this is like motor expenses. If you spend 30% of your time on the phone in connection with your business then charge 30% of:

◆ Total landline call charges
◆ Total line rental for your landline
◆ Total mobile call charges
◆ Total line rental for your mobile

If there are obvious large private calls (say in excess of £5) then exclude these from the total call expense when calculating the 30% charge.

If you have a fax line then charge 100% of fax expenses as it is difficult to convince the Inland Revenue that you own a fax machine for personal use!

Again this is not an exhaustive list. To make sure you legally maximise your allowable taxable expenditure you have to remember the following two principles:

♦ Include expenditure if it is 'wholly, necessarily and exclusively' needed for the business. If it is, include it. If it is not, exclude it or partly include it.

♦ Include a proportional amount of expenditure that is split between business and personal use, such as motor expenses and telephone calls.

Capital allowances on the cost of buying a capital asset, or a wear and tear allowance for furnished lettings

This basically means that you can either charge:

♦ 25% of the cost of any asset used to furnish the property, or
♦ 10% of the rent

as a tax-deductible expense. You cannot do both. I would always recommend doing the latter, charging 10% of the rent, because once you opt to do one or the other, you cannot change for the duration of your business. The reason I recommend 10% of the rent is because 10% of the rent is likely to be greater than 25% of the cost of the asset. If this is not the case now it will probably be the case in the future. It is better to suffer the lower deductible expense now for the benefit in the future.

You can still claim capital allowances for any asset that you use in the business, such as motor vehicles, but it will be restricted to the business element only. So in the example above of the motor vehicle with 30% business use, a car used in the business costing £5,000 would attract the following relief:

$$30\% \times 25\% \times £5,000 = £375.$$

You can never charge the cost of an item that you intend to use for longer than one year against your rental income. Anything purchased for the use of longer than one year is deemed to be an asset and only 25% of the cost can be charged each year.

Capital Gains Tax

This tax only arises when you sell the property. The capital gain is worked out as:

Sale price − purchase price = Capital Gain

The sale price is deemed to be the price achieved after deducting estate agent costs, solicitors' fees and any other expenses that were incurred wholly, necessarily and exclusively in the sale of the property.

The purchase price is the cost of the property plus all survey and legal costs.

How to reduce your Capital Gain

The way to reduce your capital gain is to understand the capital gain calculation. If you dispose of a property the following calculation will be made to work out your capital gain:

	Sale price		£125,000
Minus	Allowable costs		*£100,000*
	Purchase price	£80,000	
	(a) Incidental costs of purchase	£2,000	
	(b) Home improvements	£15,000	
	(c) Costs of establishing or defending title	£1,000	
	(d) Selling costs	£2,000	
Equals	Chargeable gain		£25,000

The sale price and the purchase price are fixed. You cannot change what you sold the property for or what you paid for it.

Allowable costs

To reduce your capital gain you have to maximise the other allowable costs. Let's look at the other allowable costs and what you can include. This part is paraphrased from the Inland Revenue itself:

Allowable costs	What you can include
(a) Incidental costs of purchase	◆ fees, commission or remuneration paid for professional advice
	◆ the costs of transferring the property
	◆ stamp duty
	◆ the costs of advertising to find a seller
	◆ the costs of any valuations needed to work out your chargeable gain (but not the costs of resolving any disagreement with the Inland Revenue about your valuations)
(b) Home improvements	These are costs which
	◆ you incurred for the purpose of enhancing the value of the property, and
	◆ are still reflected in the state or nature of the property at the date of its disposal
	You may not claim the cost of normal maintenance and repairs
(c) Costs of establishing or defending title	◆ fees, commission or remuneration paid for professional advice
(d) Selling costs	◆ fees, commission or remuneration paid for professional advice
	◆ the costs of transferring the property
	◆ the costs of advertising to find a buyer
	◆ the costs of any valuations needed to work out your chargeable gain (but not the costs of resolving any disagreement with the Inland Revenue about your valuations)

So in a nutshell you can include:

◆ Solicitor costs
◆ Accountancy fees
◆ Mortgage broker fees
◆ Redemption penalties on cleared mortgages

- Stamp duty
- Advertising
- Estate agent fees
- Valuations needed to calculate your gain
- Any improvements that still remain in the property
- Legal costs in defending your title to the property

So the first part of reducing your capital gain is to include ALL costs involved with the purchase, ownership period and sale of the property that fall within the definitions stated by the Inland Revenue. But it doesn't stop there! You can obtain further relief on the gain. Read on.

Taper relief
You can reduce your calculated gain by up to 40%. Look at this table:

Number of whole years the property has been owned	Gain remaining chargeable (%)
Less than 1	100
1	100
2	100
3	95
4	90
5	85
6	80
7	75
8	70
9	65
10 or more	60

The longer you have owned the property the less gain you have to pay. So in reference to the table above, after three complete years of ownership you start to attract taper relief. After ten years or more you attract the maximum amount of relief where only 60% of the gain is chargeable or in other words a 40% discount on the gain chargeable.

Please note it has to be complete years. So another way to reduce your capital gain is, if possible, stall your purchase to capture another year. Look at this example:

Harry has found a buyer for his investment property that he has owned for 5 years 11 months. The capital gain on the sale is £100,000. If he sells straight away then from looking at the table, 85% of the gain is chargeable, as he is deemed to have owned the asset for five complete years, equating to £85,000. However if he stalls the sale, one month later he is deemed to have owned the asset for six complete years so, looking at the table, only 80% of the gain is chargeable equating to £80,000. This method only works for assets being sold that have been owned for between two and nine years. Otherwise it makes no difference.

Personal allowance

You can still reduce your gain further. Everybody gets a Capital Gains Tax allowance of £7,900 per tax year rising year on year with inflation. So if you have a gain of £10,000 then it is reduced by £7,900 to £2,100.

If you are selling a couple of properties then try to straddle the sales either side of 5 April, the end of the tax year. This way you can apply your Capital Gains allowance for the tax year prior to 5 April on one of the properties and your Capital Gains allowance for the tax year after 5 April for the other property. This way you can make full use of your yearly allowances.

There is one final way of reducing your capital gain – Principal Place of Residence.

Principal Place of Residence (PPR)

Your own personal residence is not liable for Capital Gains Tax so any gain you make is all yours. If part of your strategy is to let out your home and move into another home and you sell your PPR within three years of leaving it then there is no tax to pay! If you sell after the three years then you still get relief for three years. Let's look at this example:

Roger lives in a house that has been his personal place of residence for eight years since he bought it, but decides to move out and rent it out. If he sells two years after he rented it out there is no tax to pay. If he sells it five years later then only:

(5–3)/13 of the gain is chargeable.

The equation being:

(Amount of years rented − 3 years)/Period of ownership.

SIPP AND FURBS

You may have heard of these terms in connection with properties and pensions. Let me explain their relevance to this subject.

SIPP

This stands for Self Invested Personal Pension. The reason why it is mentioned is that you can buy *commercial* property within this pension and enjoy all the tax breaks a normal pension has. The reason why a SIPP is not applicable in the buy-to-let situation is because we are investing in *residential* property. Residential property is not allowed under the SIPP scheme.

Commercial property is not as attractive as residential property. The reasons being:

◆ The yields are lower

◆ Borrowing is restricted to 70% loan to value

◆ Business risk is doubled – you are reliant on your tenant's business to trade well out of your property as well as having the normal risks associated with owning the commercial property itself

This is my own personal opinion. You may think that commercial property is for you. If you do get in to this game I would seriously consider investing in commercial property under this umbrella of a SIPP as the shelter to tax is quite significant.

FURBS

This stands for a Funded Unapproved Retirement Benefit Scheme. Its main beneficiaries are the higher rate tax payers only. So if you're not a higher rate tax payer and don't expect to be one then ignore this bit.

If you buy a residential property under this umbrella then:

◆ Profits from the scheme are taxed at 22% rather than 40% if you are a higher rate tax payer.

◆ Capital gains tax is 34% in comparison to 40%. A FURBS also attracts the normal taper relief explained above.

◆ You can pass a FURBS down to your family. There is no Inheritance tax to pay when passed on after death as opposed to being subject to the normal inheritance tax limits (currently £259,000). A traditional pension fund cannot be passed down.

◆ There is no limit on the contributions to a FURBS but you do not get any tax relief on your contributions.

◆ The whole fund can be withdrawn tax free compared to a traditional pension fund being restricted to 25%.

◆ Retirement can be even after the age of 75. Traditional pension funds are restricted to age 75.

The two key things you need to consider deciding on whether to invest in property using a FURBS is:

1. You can only access the money at retirement. If you want to retire prior to normal retirement age then it's not possible under this scheme. A FURBS restricts your freedom. Once you invest your money in a FURBS you can't get at it till retirement.

2. There are administration costs involved. You have to use an accountant and the accounting for such a scheme has to be spot on.

Personally I like the freedom that I have. Maybe when I'm over 45 and if FURBS are still about then I'll consider one. I think if your target earning is more than £50,000 p.a. profit from property, you don't require any of this £50,000+ p.a. to live on today, and you're aged over 45 then a FURBS may be for you. Seek professional advice.

Legal Aspects

The legal aspects a landlord faces can be split into three broad categories:

◆ Contractual
◆ Regulatory
◆ All-encompassing

CONTRACTUAL

Contractual refers to the legal contracts that you will sign and enter into. You will be bound to fulfil your obligations under the terms of the contract. Breach of terms can result in you being sued and ultimately paying damages to the aggrieved party. As a landlord you will enter into legal contracts with your:

◆ Lender
◆ Tenant
◆ Insurer
◆ Letting agent

Lender

Prior to entering into a contract with a lender, the lender has to know about you. The lender asks you a number of questions and expects the truth. If it found that you have misled the lender by any of your answers to their questions, they can demand repayment of the loan in full plus all recovery costs. They can also inform the police and charge you with obtaining finance by deception. This is fraud and you can go to prison.

Once the lender has established that you are a person worth lending to, the lender insists you sign their contract. The lender sets the terms of the contract. As the lender is lending money to you it is their right to set the terms of the contract. Unless you are borrowing a large sum of money then you can never include any clauses in the contract based on your terms – that's just the way it is. The key terms of the contract are:

◆ Payment – You have to pay the mortgage repayments on the dates the lender dictates. If you fail to do so, the lender can repossess the property.

◆ Maintenance – You must keep the property in a good state of repair fit enough to be habitable.

◆ Occupation – You must not leave the property vacant for more than 30 days.

Tenant

There are several legal documents that are created when you find a suitable tenant:

◆ An inventory
◆ An Assured Shorthold Tenancy Agreement
◆ An eviction order

An inventory

An inventory is a list of all items that are in the property – it includes descriptions of items, quantities and condition. Both the tenant and the landlord should sign this list. When the tenant decides to leave the property you can check the list to see what is left in the property. If there are any deviations from the list you can charge the tenant to correct the deviation. So, for example, if there were four dining chairs when the tenant moved in and now there are only three, you can deduct the cost of replacing the dining chair from the tenant's deposit.

If you get an inventory done it will ensure that the tenant thinks that you care about the place you are letting and the tenant will be less likely to damage the property. If the condition of the carpet is recorded then the tenant is more likely to remove any stains caused, as he fears that you will deduct cleaning costs from his deposit.

Professional inventory services can be found in the Yellow Pages or by visiting www.yell.com.

An Assured Shorthold Tenancy Agreement (AST)

This is an agreement between the landlord and tenant. It binds both parties to certain duties and obligations. The main features of a tenancy agreement are:

- **Rent** – How much rent is to be paid and the frequency of payment.

- **Duration** – An AST is for a minimum of six months and maximum of twelve months. I would always suggest a tenancy of six months as the tenant has the right to run the duration of the tenancy unless there is a breach on either party. See below.

- **Running expenses** – It sets out who is liable for the running expenses of the property.

- **Tenant obligations** – It details the tenant's obligations to the property and the landlord, such as maintenance, not to sublet, informing the landlord of problems in good time, and reporting damage.

- **Landlord obligations** – It details the landlord's obligations to the property and the tenant, such as privacy and timeliness of repairs.

Both the tenant and the landlord have to sign, with both signatures witnessed by an independent third party.

In Appendix 5 is an example of an Assured Shorthold Tenancy Agreement.

An eviction order

A landlord can serve this notice and give a minimum of two months, notice to the tenant for the following main reasons:

1. You wish to reside in the property
2. Non-payment of rent
3. Mortgagees wishing to repossess

In Appendix 6 is an example of a Notice of Intention to Seek Possession (Section 21).

If the tenant doesn't leave then:

1. File copies of the notices sent to the tenant with the court. Sue for all rent arrears and legal costs and court fees.

2. Wait for 14 days for the tenant to reply.

3. If no response is made (which is likely) then a possession order is made giving 14 days' notice.

4. If the tenants don't leave then call the police to evict them as they are now in your property unlawfully.

We have to face a reality here though. This procedure will take a long time, give you stress and you can potentially lose up to six months' rent. If you include court fees and solicitors' costs and the threat of damage to your property the whole eviction process could cost you in excess of £3,000. If you want the tenant out of your property and they have ignored all your notices then offer to pay them to leave. This option could be cheaper. I would suggest one month's rent as fair. This will pay the deposit for their next property.

Try to initiate a friendly separation. Do not add fuel to an already fiery situation by losing your temper and threatening immediate court action. Statistically only three per cent of tenants tend to be bad tenants – bad tenants being tenants who have no intention of paying the rent, not tenants who lose their job and can't pay their rent. If a tenant loses their job it is more than likely that they are going to get another job. If they have been relatively good payers of the rent then be patient with them.

In my experience I would say that the three per cent statistic is right. The majority of people wish to settle in a home and feel secure. The best way for them to feel secure is to pay their rent on time.

Insurer

You will have to enter legal contracts with insurance companies to cover you against certain risks. Your insurance will only ever be valid if you have originally told the truth on your proposal form when obtaining the insurance. The main insurances you will take out when investing in property will be:

- ◆ Buildings insurance – The insurance you pay to cover the property against fire, vandalism, water damage or weather damage.

- ◆ Contents insurance – This is insurance for items such as carpets, furniture and other fittings that you have provided for the property.

- ◆ Rental guarantee – This is insurance against your tenant defaulting on the rental payments.

- ◆ Emergency assistance – This insurance will cover the costs of any emergency repairs that have to be carried out including all call-out charges.

When filling out the form they will ask you about previous claims. If you have any previous claims then reveal them. If you do have to make a claim and you have not told them about a previous claim then they do not have to pay out. It is very easy for them to find out if you have had a claim as they have a central register of all claims paid out.

If you do lie and they catch you out you will find it difficult to get insurance in the future, as you may be put on a blacklist which is accessible to all insurers.

Letting agents

If you do decide to use a letting agent then you have to read their terms and conditions very carefully. Watch for:

◆ Timeliness of payment – Check to see how soon the letting agent has to hand over the money, once the tenant has received it. I would not accept any period longer than three days.

◆ Get out clauses – If you decide to no longer use the letting agent check to see how easy it is to get out. One agent tried to sue me for all the lost commission he would have earned even though I was now collecting the rent! If you have an idea of using a letting agent at first and then taking over in six months inform the letting agent of this intention. You may be able to strike a deal where you have a realistically priced option to get out of the contract.

REGULATIONS GOVERNING THE RENTING OF PROPERTIES

There are there three main regulations governing the renting of properties:

◆ Gas safety
◆ Electrical safety
◆ Fire resistance

Gas safety

If there is gas at the property then you have to get an annual landlord's safety record from a CORGI registered engineer. They will inspect:

◆ The central heating boiler
◆ Oven and hob

- Gas fire
- Gas meters

If you do not get one of these certificates and someone suffers or even dies from carbon monoxide poisoning then you could face a hefty fine and imprisonment. The guilt will be even worse.

Electrical safety

A yearly inspection is advisable, but not a legal requirement, for all electrical appliances supplied with the property by an NICEIC contractor. Basically anything electrical will need to be examined and passed by the NICEIC contractor.

So it's quite obvious – keep the number of electrical items to a minimum! The fewer electrical items you supply the less there is likely to go wrong. This limits the reasons why your tenant can ring you up telling you about a problem. You don't need your tenant ringing you up at 6a.m. complaining about the kettle not working.

There is no certificate issued but an inspection will cover you from being sued if any electrical appliance were to harm your tenants or their guests.

Fire resistance

All upholstered furniture must comply with the Furniture and Furnishings (fire) (safety) Regulations 1988. You can tell if the furniture is compliant because there will be a label in the cushioning. Any furniture purchased after 1990 will automatically comply with all fire regulations.

Although not a legal requirement, I would recommend that smoke alarms be installed in rented properties to cover you against any negligence claim if you were to be sued.

ALL-ENCOMPASSING LAWS OF THE LAND

You will also be legally bound by the normal all-encompassing laws of the land. This includes:

◆ The law of tort – negligence and personal injury
◆ Criminal law

We are all bound by the above two laws even if you are not a property investor.

The law of tort

Even though you may have all the safety records in place you still owe a duty of care to your tenant and anyone who enters your property. If it can be shown that you were negligent in any way then you could be sued and ordered to pay damages.

As a landlord you are liable for any damages if all of these conditions are satisfied:

(i)   Your tenant or anyone entering your investment property were to suffer an injury; and

(ii) You owed a duty of care to the person entering your investment property who suffered the personal injury; and

(iii) You breached that duty of care.

So for example if Zak, the landlord, failed to fix the cooker socket in the kitchen and the tenant's guest, Liz, suffered an electric shock burn then Zak would be liable to compensate Liz for her injury.

This is because:

(i)   Liz suffered injury;

(ii) Zak owed a duty of care as it is realistically to be expected that a tenant would invite a guest into their property;

(iii) Zak breached that duty of care, as he did not fix the socket when asked to by the tenant.

Criminal law

Even if your tenant hasn't paid you any rent for two months you cannot 'send the boys round'. Threatening your tenant or being violent to your tenant because he hasn't paid you any rent is no justification for your behaviour in the eyes of the law. Investing in property can sometimes challenge your ability to remain calm and situations can become quite heated. You have to be a responsible person and realise that if you want to build a property pension seriously then you have to act lawfully in every way.

Appendix 1

GLOSSARY

Annuity – An income that is provided to you till death. An annuity is purchased with the proceeds from your traditional pension fund.

Gearing – Gearing an investment simply means borrowing to acquire the investment. The higher the gearing the higher the investment.

Interest only mortgage – A mortgage where you only pay the interest of the amount borrowed and then settle the balance in full at the end of the mortgage term.

LTV – Loan to Value. The loan is expressed as a percentage of the purchase price or valuation, so a loan of £75,000 on a property costing £100,000 is a 75% LTV loan.

Pension – The income receivable after you have stopped work.

Property pension – A fund invested in property that delivers an income from the rent derived from these properties.

Repayment mortgage – A mortgage where you pay the interest and the capital over the duration of the mortgage. This type of mortgage ensures that you pay off the mortgage at the end of the term.

Traditional pension fund – A fund that has amassed from your contributions invested in shares and cash.

Void period – The period when no monies are received, i.e. when the property is empty.

Yield – This is the annual rental income expressed as a percentage of the total purchase price of the property.

Appendix 2

HIGHER RATE TAX PAYER CALCULATIONS
Traditional pension contribution table

Age	Personal contribution	Government contribution 40% (tax)	Value of year's contribution at age 65
41	1,200	480	5,632
42	1,251	500	5,592
43	1,304	522	5,552
44	1,360	544	5,512
45	1,417	567	5,473
46	1,478	591	5,434
47	1,540	616	5,395
48	1,606	642	5,357
49	1,674	670	5,318
50	1,745	698	5,280
51	1,819	728	5,243
52	1,897	759	5,205
53	1,977	791	5,168
54	2,061	825	5,131
55	2,149	860	5,094
56	2,240	896	5,058
57	2,336	934	5,022
58	2,435	974	4,986
59	2,538	1,015	4,950
60	2,646	1,058	4,915
61	2,759	1,103	4,880
62	2,876	1,150	4,845
63	2,998	1,199	4,810
64	3,126	1,250	4,776
65	3,258	1,303	4,742
	51,692	20,677	129,371

Income from annuity

$$£45.78 \times £129,371/1000 = \textbf{£5,922.60 p.a.} \text{ (say £5,923)}$$

Summary

What you put in	Total pension contributions for the 25 years	£51,692
What you get out	Annual income from the annuity till death	£5,923 p.a. till death

PROPERTY PENSION

Property		1	2	3	4	
	Yrs 0–5	Yrs 6–10	Yrs 11–15	Yrs 16–20	Yrs 21–25	Yrs 26 onwards
Purchase price		30,000				
Deposit (15% of purchase price)		4,500				
Debt		25,500				
Rent (8% yield)		2,400	3,063	3,909	4,989	6,368
Interest (5% APR)		1,275	1,275	1,275	1,275	1,275
Other costs (20% of rent)		480	613	782	998	1,274
Net inflow before tax		645	1,175	1,852	2,717	3,819
After tax **(40% higher rate)**		387	705	1,111	1,630	2,292
Fees		1,500				
Total deposit and fees		6,000				
Purchase price			38,288			
Deposit (15% of purchase price)			5,743			
Debt			32,545			
Rent (8% yield)			3,063	3,909	4,989	6,368
Interest (5% APR)			1,627	1,627	1,627	1,627
Other costs (20% of rent)			613	782	998	1,274
Net inflow before tax			823	1,500	2,364	3,467
After tax **(40% higher rate)**			494	900	1,419	2,080
Fees			2,000			
Total deposit and fees			7,743			

Property	1	2	3	4	
Purchase price			48,867		
Deposit (15% of purchase price)			7,330		
Debt			41,537		
Rent (8% yield)			3,909	4,989	6,368
Interest (5% APR)			2,077	2,077	2,078
Other costs (20% of rent)			782	998	1,274
Net inflow before tax			1,051	1,915	3,016
After tax **(40% higher rate)**			630	1,149	1,810
Fees			2,500		
Total Deposit and Fees			9,830		
Purchase price			62,368		
Deposit (15% of purchase price)			9,355		
Debt			53,013		
Rent (8% yield)			4,989	6,368	
Interest (5% APR)			2,651	2,651	
Other costs (20% of rent)			998	1,274	
Net inflow before tax			1,341	2,443	
After tax **(40% higher)**			805	1,466	
Fees			3,000		
Total deposit and fees			12,355		
Annual profit inflow	387	1,199	2,642	5,002	7,648

Property	Age	Deposit and fees (outflow)	Profit (inflow)	Net outflow	Purchase price (5% growth p.a.)	Property value at age 65	Debt (mortgage)	Net Value
	41							
	42							
	43							
	44							
1	45	6,000			30,000	83,579	25,500	58,079
	46	0	387					
	47	0	387					
	48	0	387					
	49	0	387					
2	50	7,743	387		38,288	83,579	32,545	51,034
	51	0	1,199					
	52	0	1,199					
	53	0	1,199					
	54	0	1,199					
3	55	9,830	1,199		48,867	83,579	41,537	42,042
	56	0	2,642					
	57	0	2,642					
	58	0	2,642					
	59	0	2,642					
4	60	12,355	2,642		62,368	83,579	53,013	30,566
	61	0	5,002					
	62	0	5,002					
	63	0	5,002					
	64	0	5,002					
	65	0	5,002					
		35,928	46,151	−10,223	179,523	334,316	152,595	181,721

Summary

What you put in	Deposit and Fees less profits from the properties over the 25 years	−£10,223 (say Nil)
What you get out	Profits for years 26 onwards	£7,648 p.a. forever

If you wish to sell the portfolio to purchase an annuity then there is no difference if you are a higher rate tax payer as all gains are subject to Capital Gains Tax of 40%.

So the table for a higher rate tax payer would be:

	Traditional pension	Property pension (buy and hold)	Property pension (buy and sell)
What you put in	£51,692	Nil	Nil
What you get out	£5,119 p.a. till death	£7,648 p.a. forever	£6,618.44 p.a. till death

So a property pension is still better than a traditional pension even if you are a higher rate tax payer.

Appendix 3

8%+ YIELDING AREAS

All these areas of England, Scotland and Wales offer yields of greater than 8%. This ensures that you keep your personal contribution to a minimum and improves your ability to weather interest rate rises, voids and repairs.

SOUTH WEST ENGLAND

Avon, Bristol

Axminster, Devon

Bodmin, Cornwall

Bovey Tracey, Devon

Bridgewater, Taunton

Callington, Cornwall

Chard, Somerset

Chelston, Torquay, Devon

Clevedon, Bristol

Dawlish, Devon

Devonport, Plymouth

Filton, Bristol

Gillingham, Dorset

Honicknowle, Plymouth

Hooe, Plymouth

Houndstone, Somerset

Ilfracombe, Devon

Ilminster, Somerset

Keyham, Plymouth

Laira, Plymouth

Launceston, Cornwall

Lipson, Plymouth

Looe, Cornwall

Paignton, Devon

Plymouth City Centre, Plymouth

St Budeaux, Plymouth

Shepton Mallet, Somerset

Stoke, Plymouth

Stratton Creber, Newquay

Tavistock, Devon

Teignmouth, Devon

Topsham, Devon

Torquay, Devon

Wellington, Somerset

Westbury, Bath

Weston Super Mare, Somerset

Yeovil, Somerset

SOUTH EAST ENGLAND

Ashford, Kent
Broadstairs, Kent
Canterbury, Kent
Chatham, Kent
Cliftonville, Kent
Dartford, Kent
Dover, Kent
Eastbourne, Sussex
Erith, Kent
Faversham, Kent

Folkstone, Kent
Hastings, East Sussex
Herne Bay, Kent
Margate, Kent
Ramsgate, Kent
Rochester, Kent
Sittingbourne, Kent
Snodland, Kent
Westgate-on-sea, Kent

SOUTHERN ENGLAND

Bexhill-on-sea, Sussex
Bognor Regis, West Sussex
Bournemouth, Dorset
Fareham, Hampshire
Rottingdean, Brighton
Rowner, Gosport
Ryde, Isle Of Wight
St Leonards-on-sea, East Sussex

St Marys, Southampton
Sandown, Isle Of Wight
Shirley, Southampton
Sholing, Southampton
Southbourne, Dorset
Southsea, Hampshire
Thornhill, Southampton

ESSEX, HERTS AND MIDDLESEX

Aveley, Essex
Basildon, Essex
Clacton-on-sea, Essex
Colchester, Essex
Dagenham, Essex
East Tilbury, Essex
Enfield, Middlesex
Frinton-on-sea, Essex
Grays, Essex
Halstead, Essex
Harlow, Essex

Harold Hill, Essex
Harwich, Essex
Hornchurch, Essex
Laindon, Essex
Pitsea, Essex
Purfleet, Essex
Rainham, Essex
Romford, Essex
Sawbridgeworth, Herts
Sheerness, Essex
Shoeburyness, Essex

South Ockendon, Essex
Southend, Essex
Stanford le Hope, Essex
Tilbury, Essex

Waltham Cross, Essex
Westcliffe-on-sea, Essex
Wickford, Essex
Witham, Essex

LONDON

Beckton
Bexley Heath
Leyton
Northolt
Plaistow

Streatham
Thamesmead
Walthamstow
West Hendon
Woolwich

EAST ANGLIA

Attleborough, Norfolk
Boston, Lincs.
Brookenby, Lincs.
Bungay, Norfolk
Chatteris, Cambs.
Cromer, Norfolk
Downham Market, Norfolk
Eye, Suffolk
Grantham, Lincs.
Hadleigh, Suffolk
Ipswich, Suffolk
Kings Lynn, Norfolk
Lincoln, Lincs.

Market Rasen, Lincs.
Mundesley, Norfolk
Norwich, Norfolk
Orton Goldhay, Peterborough
Orton Malbourne, Peterborough
St Neots, Cambs.
Skegness, Lincs.
Sudbury, Suffolk
Welland, Peterborough
Wickham Market, Woodbridge,
    Suffolk
Wisbech, Cambs.

THE MIDLANDS

Anstey Heights, Leicester
Aspley, Notts.
Bedford, Bedfordshire
Bestwood, Notts.
Bilborough, Notts.
Binley, Coventry

Bobbersmill, Notts.
Braunstone, Leicester
Broxtowe, Notts.
Bulwell, Notts.
Burton-on-Trent, Staffs.
Camphill, Coventry

Clifton, Notts.
Corby, Northants.
Daventry, Warwickshire
Dunstable, Bedfordshire
Foleshill, Coventry
Highbury Vale, Notts.
Hodge Hill, Birmingham
Ilkeston, Notts.
Irthlingborough, Northants.
Kettering, Northants.
Kimberley, Notts.
Kirkby-in-Ashfield, Notts.
Leicester City Centre, Leicester
Luton, Bedfordshire
Mansfield, Notts.
Moulton, Northants.
Newark, Notts.
Newcastle-under-Lyme, Staffs.
Newstead Village, Hucknall, Notts.

Northampton, Northants.
Oldbury, West Midlands
Rednal, Birmingham
Rugby, Warwickshire
Rushden, Northants.
Shrewsbury
Stoke-on-Trent, Staffs.
Strelley, Notts.
Sutton-in-Ashfield, Notts.
The Meadows, Notts.
Thorneywood, Notts.
Thorpelands, Northants.
Top Valley, Notts.
Walsall, West Midlands
Warren Hill, Notts.
Wellingborough, Northants.
Willenhall, Coventry
Wolverhampton, West Midlands

THE WEST

Caldicot, Gloucs.
Churchdown, Gloucs.
Cinderford, Gloucs.
Coleford, Gloucs.
Hardwicke, Gloucs.
Hereford, Herefordshire

Kidderminster, Worcs.
Newtown Farm, Herefordshire
Redditch, Worcs.
Tewkesbury, Gloucs.
Worcester, Worcs.

THE MID-NORTH

Balby, Doncaster
Beeston, Leeds
Castleford
Crossgates, Leeds
Dewsbury

Garforth
Goole
Grimsby, Yorkshire
Huddersfield, Yorkshire
Hull

Marsden, Yorkshire
Pocklington, Yorkshire
Rochdale, Lancs.
Rotherham
Roundhay

Scarborough, Yorkshire
Scunthorpe
Skipton, Bradford
Wakefield, Yorkshire

NORTH WEST ENGLAND

Accrington
Allerton, Liverpool
Bacup, Manchester
Barnsley, Lancs.
Birkenhead, Lancs.
Blackburn
Blackpool
Bolton
Bootle, Liverpool
Bradford
Broughton, Cheshire
Bury, Lancs.
Chester, Cheshire
Clayton, Manchester
Colne, Lancs.
Crewe, Cheshire
Darwen, Lancs.
Denton, Manchester
Derby
Dudley
Eccles, Manchester
Eddington, Doncaster
Farnworth, Lancs.
Gainsborough, Manchester
Golborne, Cheshire
Halifax
Holywell, Flintshire

Huyton, Prescot
Hyde Park, Manchester
Keighley
Kirkby, Maghull
Leigh, Lancs.
Liverpool L4
Liverpool L6
Liverpool L7
Liverpool L8
Liverpool L9
Liverpool L13
Liverpool L14
Liverpool L20
Longsight, Manchester
Mexborough
Morecombe, Lancs.
Moss Side, Manchester
Northwich, Cheshire
Openshaw, Manchester
Peasley Cross, Merseyside
Preston
Rishton, Lancs
Rock Ferry, Bebington
Rotherham
Runcorn, Cheshire
Rusholme, Manchester
St Helens, Merseyside

Salford, Manchester
Sheffield City Centre
Swinton, Manchester
Wallasey
Walton Vale, Lancs
Warrington, Lancs
Waterloo, Lancs

West Derby
Wigan
Winsford, Cheshire
Withlington, Manchester
Wombwell
Worksop, Manchester
Worsley, Manchester

NORTH EAST

Arthurs Hill, Newcastle
Benwell, Newcastle
Bishop Auckland, Darlington
Blakelaw, West Denton
Blyth, Newcastle
Carlisle, Northumberland
Chilton, Darlington
Colliery Row, Durham
Consett
Elswick, Tyne and Wear
Ferryhill, Spennymoor
Gateshead, Newcastle
Hartlepool
Hebburn, Tyne and Wear
Hendon, Sunderland
Hexham, Northumberland

Houghton-le-Spring, Durham
Lemington, West Denton
Middlesbrough, Cleveland
Newcastle-upon-Tyne,
   Northumberland
Newton Aycliffe, Darlington
Prudhoe, Northumberland
Redcar, Cleveland
Ryton, Crawcrook
Seaham, Durham
South Shields, Newcastle
Stockton-on-Tees, Cleveland
Walkergate, Tyne and Wear
Wallsend, Newcastle
Washington, Tyne and Wear

WALES

Abercynon, Pontypridd
Abertillery, Ebbw Vale
Caerphilly
Church Village, Pontypridd
Edwardsville, Pontypridd
Ely, Rhiwbina

Gilfach Goch, Pontypridd
Greenfield Terrace, Ebbw Vale
Neath, Glamorgan
Port Talbot, Glamorgan
Treharris, Pontypridd

SCOTLAND

Airdrie, Lanarkshire

Alexandria, Dumbarton

Beith, Bridge of Weir

Bellshill, Lanarkshire

Bridgeton, Glasgow

Broxburn, Livingston

Carstairs Junction, Lanarkshire

Chapelhall, Airdrie

Cleland, Lanarkshire

Craigshill, Livingston

Cronberry, Ayr

Dalry, Bridge of Weir

Darvel, Kilmarnock

Dennistown, Glasgow

Dumbarton, Dumbartonshire

East Kilbride, Glasgow

Falkirk, East Lothian

Glengarnock, Bridge of Weir

Glenrothes, East Lothian

Greenock, Refrewshire

Govanhill, Glasgow

Hamilton, Lanarkshire

Ibrox, Glasgow

Inverheithing, Dalgety Bay

Kilbirnie, Bridge of Weir

Kilsyth, Glasgow

Kilwinning, Troon

Kirkcaldy, East Lothian

Kirkintolloch, Bishopbriggs

Lochgelly, Dumfermline

Maybole, Ayr

New Cumnock, Ayr

Newmilus, Kilmarnock, Ayrshire

North Carbrain, Cumberland

Paisley, Renfrewshire

Port Glasgow, Refrewshire

Priesthill, Glasgow

Saracen Cross, Glasgow

Springboig, Glasgow

Stewarton, Kilmarnock

Tollcross, Glasgow

Whitburn, Livingston

Wishaw, Lanarkshire

Yoker, Glasgow

Appendix 4

PROPERTY WEBSITES

The list of websites below enables you to search for properties in the area you are interested in. All these sites direct you ultimately to the estate agent that is selling the property. There are also rental sites included in this list so you can keep abreast of the current market rental values of properties you have or are currently interested in.

I personally use rightmove.co.uk, ukpropertyshop.com, asserta.com and home.co.uk to find my properties. These sites seem professionally run and have a large database of properties for sale.

Sales and rental websites

www.rightmove.co.uk

www.asserta.co.uk

www.08004homes.com

www.home.co.uk

www.accommodation.com

www.national-property-register.
   co.uk

www.themovechannel.com

www.accommodation-directory.
   co.uk

www.fish4homes.co.uk

www.homesdujour.com

www.housedeals.co.uk

www.propertyfinder.co.uk

www.mondial-property.co.uk

www.numberone4property.co.uk

www.primelocation.com

www.propertyads-online.com

www.propertyfile.co.uk

www.propertylive.co.uk

www.saleourproperty.com

www.ukpg.co.uk

www.ukpropertyguide.co.uk

www.underoneroof.com

www.wheretolive.co.uk

www.froglet.com

www.move.co.uk

www.halfapercent.com

www.p4L.co.uk
www.londonpropertyguide.co.uk
www.cdproperty.co.uk
www.propertydirect.co.uk
www.rentalsandsales.co.uk
www.estates-directory.co.uk
www.ukhomesguide.co.uk
www.accommodatingcompany.co.uk
www.home-sale.co.uk
www.housesearchuk.co.uk
www.lookproperty.co.uk
www.ukhousesales.co.uk
www.londonshome.co.uk
www.propertymatters.co.uk
www.bainprop.co.uk

www.haylingproperty.co.uk
www.foxtons.co.uk
www.shobrook.co.uk
www.palmsagency.co.uk
www.jtrproperty.co.uk
www.coppingjoyce.co.uk
www.milburys.co.uk
www.davisestates.co.uk
www.stonegateestates.co.uk
www.forgetestateagents.co.uk
www.nicholasirwin.co.uk
www.ashtons.co.uk
www.claridges-estates.co.uk
www.pfivales.co.uk
www.bansale.estates.co.uk
www.dauntons.co.uk
www.stratfordproperty.co.uk

Sales only websites

www.propertyworld.co.uk
www.smartestates.com
www.stoptolook.co.uk
www.uk-property-sale-directory.co.uk
www.daltons.co.uk
www.homehunter.co.uk
www.homepages.co.uk
www.homes-uk.co.uk/hfs_home_uke.html
www.homeselluk.com
www.hotproperty.co.uk
www.house-directory.co.uk
www.thehousehunter.co.uk/default.asp
www.housenet.co.uk

www.houseweb.co.uk
www.thelondonoffice.co.uk
www.newhomesnetwork.co.uk
www.properties-direct.com
www.reale-state.co.uk
www.smartnewhomes.com
www.uk-property.com
www.ukpropertysales.net
www.wwpc.uk.com
www.your-move.co.uk
www.fairview.co.uk
www.assertahome.com
www.ukpropertyshop.co.uk
www.partake.co.uk
www.property-sight.co.uk
www.prestigeproperty.co.uk

www.tspc.co.uk

www.homesalez.com

www.hotproperties2000.co.uk

www.your-life.co.uk

www.agentfreesales.co.uk

www.propertysales.co.uk

www.globalmart.co.uk

www.propertyfinderwales.co.uk

www.paramount-properties.co.uk

www.estate-agent-property.co.uk

www.webhouses.co.uk

www.property-go.co.uk

www.capital-residence.co.uk

www.michaeltucker.co.uk

www.toplondonproperties.co.uk

www.carltons-dundee.co.uk

www.howards.co.uk

www.owner-property-sales.co.uk

www.property4uk.co.uk

www.smithvalentine.demon.co.uk

www.jparissteele.co.uk

www.villagategroup.com

www.wisemove.co.uk

www.dmea.co.uk

www.gatehouseestates.co.uk

www.andrewpontin.co.uk

www.walsall-estates.co.uk

www.stewartwatson.co.uk

www.newey.co.uk

www.hamiltonbrooks.co.uk

www.bennettjones.co.uk

www.pro-net.co.uk

www.lakewood-properties.co.uk

www.pickitts.co.uk

www.housemarket.co.uk

Rentals only websites

www.homelet.co.uk

www.rent.co.uk

www.simprent.u-net.com

www.citylet.com

www.letonthenet.com

www.letsrentuk.com

www.lettingweb.com

www.simplyrent.co.uk

www.spacetorent.com

www.studenthousehunt.com

www.studentpad.co.uk

www.palacegate.co.uk

www.excel-property.co.uk

www.assuredproprentals.co.uk

www.cambridge-rentals.co.uk

www.propertyrentals.co.uk

www.faulknerproperty.co.uk

www.flemingpropertyrentals.
  co.uk

www.enaparkinsonpropertyrentals.
  co.uk

www.the-net.co.uk

www.mossoak.co.uk

www.torent.co.uk

www.net-lettings.co.uk

www.property-go.co.uk

www.sunkissed.co.uk

www.letters.co.uk

Appendix 5

ASSURED SHORTHOLD TENANCY AGREEMENT

Here is an example of an AST.

ASSURED SHORTHOLD TENANCY AGREEMENT

1. Tenancy agreement made the day of 10th January 200X

Between   *[insert landlord's name]*

Of
                                     [insert landlord's address]

(Hereinafter called the Landlord which expression shall include the person for the time being entitled to the reversion expectant on the determination of the tenancy hereby created) of the one part

And   *[insert tenant's name]*

Of   *[insert tenant's previous address]*

(Hereinafter called the tenant which expression shall include his successors in title) of the other part.

Whereby it is agreed as follows:

The landlord lets and the tenant takes the dwelling house known as:

                        [insert investment property's address]

(Hereinafter called the premises)

Together with the furniture, fixtures and effects therein upon an Assured Shorthold Tenancy within the meaning of section 19(a) of the Housing Act 1988 as amended by the Housing Act 1996, for the period of six months starting on the 10th January 200X until 9th July 200X. The rent of £____ per week, payable clear of deductions. Any money received for payment of rent for the premises is deemed to have been received from the tenant in advance on the first day of every week, the first such payment to be payable on the signing of this contract.

---

2. The tenant agrees:

(a) To pay the rent of £_____ per week in the manner aforesaid, without any reductions whatsoever.

(b) To pay the agent upon signing hereof a deposit of £____, to be held by the landlord against liability of the tenant arising under this agreement. The landlord will provide a written list of dilapidations within 28 days of the end of the tenancy, and a further 28 days will be allowed for discussion and negotiations to arrange settlement. After this period of time either party may revert to use of the law courts to resolve the dispute. If there are no dilapidations, the landlord will undertake to return the deposit to the tenant within seven working days of the end of the tenancy.

(c) To pay all charges for gas and electric current supplied to the premises during the tenancy (all charges including any rental or other necessary charges) for use of the telephone if the tenant wishes to have the telephone connected, and the costs of reconnecting such services if they are withheld owing to the act or omission of the tenant. The tenant is also responsible for the water rates and council tax or replacement taxation for the term of the tenancy.

(d) To keep all parts of the premises, including landlord's furniture, fixtures and fittings in good and tenantable repair and in good decorative state and ventilated (fair wear and tear and damage by accidental fire, maintenance and repairs which are hereafter agreed to be done by the landlord and those which are statutory for section 11 of the Housing Act 1985 omitted); to maintain the garden to an acceptable standard.

(e) Not to assign, underlet, charge or part with or share the possession or occupation of the premises or any part thereof and not to grant any licence to occupy the premises of any part thereof.

(f) Not to use the premises or any part of for any purpose other than that of a private residence.

(g) Not to carry on upon the premises any profession, trade or business, or let apartments or rooms, or receive paying guests or lodgers or place or exhibit any notice board or notice on the premises.

(h) Not to use the premises for any illegal or immoral purpose.

(i) Not to do or permit or suffer anything in the premises (or any building of which the premises form part) which may be or grow to be a nuisance or annoyance to the landlord (or any superior landlord) or to any occupier or tenant of any part of any building of which the premises form part;

(j) Not to damage, injure, or make any alteration to the premises or any part thereof.

(k) Within seven days of receipt thereof to send all correspondence addressed to the landlord directly to the landlord whose address forms part of this tenancy agreement. Any other correspondence of unknown names should be forwarded to the landlord. This should include any notice, order or proposal relating to the premises (or any building of which the premises form part) given, made or issued under or by virtue or any statute, regulation, order, direction or by law by any competent authority.

(l) To permit the landlord upon giving 48 hours' notice (except in the case of emergency when no notice shall be required) to enter upon the premises with or without workmen and equipment and to view the state and condition thereof and, if necessary, to carry out any repairs, alterations or other works.

(m) To pay all fees, expenses and costs (including solicitors', councils', and surveyors' fees) incurred by the landlord in preparing and serving notice on the tenant of any breach of any of the covenants on the part of the tenants herein contained notwithstanding forfeiture is avoided otherwise than by relief granted by the court.

(n) To notify the landlord promptly after any event which causes damage to the premises, furniture, fixtures and fittings or which may give rise to a claim under the insurances of the premises.

(o) Not to leave the premises vacant for more than 21 consecutive days and to keep the premises locked and secured when vacant, and the tenant is responsible for using the security provided at all times.

(p) Not to change the locks to any doors of the premises, without the permission of the landlord; not to make any duplicate keys thereof but to return all such keys to the landlord at the end of the tenancy.

(q) To pay for professional cleaning redecorations, and garden maintenance should the final inventory dictate that such services are, in reasonable opinion of the landlord, necessary.

(r) Within the last two months of the tenancy to permit the landlord at reasonable hours, to enter and view the premises with prospective tenants or purchasers.

(s) At the end of the tenancy to yield up to the landlord the premises, furniture, fixtures, and effects properly repaired, decorated, and kept in accordance with the obligations hereinbefore contained, and to remove from the premises all the tenant's effects.

(t) No to remove any of the landlord's furniture, fixtures and effects from the premises, and to leave them in the same location as found.

(u) To keep the furniture, fixtures and effects in their present state of repair and condition (reasonable wear and tear and damage by accidental fire excepted) and to replace with similar articles of at least equal value, style and colour of any part of the said furniture, fixtures, fittings or effects, which may be destroyed or damaged (except as foresaid) so as to be incapable of being returned to their former condition.

(v) Not to keep any pets.

3. The landlord agrees:

(a)   That the tenant paying the rent hereby reserved and performing and observing the various agreements on their part contained herein shall peaceably hold and enjoy the premises during the tenancy without any interruption by the landlord or any person claiming under or in trust for them.

(b)   To carry out those repairs, liability for which is cast upon the landlord by sections 11–16 inclusive of the Landlord and Tenant Act 1985 as amended by Section 116 of The Housing Act 1988.

(c)   To pay the ground rent, service charges, and all sums payable by the landlord herein to the head landlord under the terms of the head lease.

(d)   To insure the premises against loss or damage by fire, explosion, and such additional risks as the landlord may deem desirable.

4. The landlord and tenant agree:

(a)   If the rent hereby reserved or any part thereof shall be unpaid for 14 days after becoming payable (whether being formally demanded or not) or if any covenant or agreement on the tenant's part herein contained shall not be performed or observed then in any of the said cases it shall be lawful for the landlord at any time thereafter to re-enter upon the premises or any part thereof in the name of the whole and thereupon the tenancy shall absolutely determine but without prejudice to the rights of the landlord in respect of any breach of the tenant's covenants or agreements herein.

(b)   Ownership of all property left at the premises at the end of the tenancy shall immediately pass to the landlord who shall be entitled (though not bound) to sell the same for their own benefit and where necessary make charge upon to the tenant or the tenant's deposit to refund any additional costs not recouped within the values received for the said articles.

(c)   Where the landlord or the tenant consist of more than one person, the covenants on their part in this agreement shall be joint and several.

(d)   Any notices served by the landlord on the tenant shall be sufficiently served if sent by second-class post or delivered by hand to the tenant at the premises or the last known address of the tenant.

(e)   To end the tenancy at or after six months, either party must give at least two months' prior notice in writing.

(f)   In the event of maintenance that requires immediate attention outside office hours, and falls under the landlord's statutory responsibilities under section 11 of the Housing Act 1985, the tenant may spend up to £50 to minimise damage or effect a repair without reference to the landlord, but should inform the landlord at the earliest opportunity. Any other repairs of any nature must be referred to the landlord or landlord's agent. Any other repairs authorised by the tenant will be the responsibility of the tenant to pay.

It is hereby agreed that the parties hereto witness the day and year first above written.

AS WITNESS the hands of the parties hereto the day and year first above written.

SIGNED by the above named _____
(The landlord)

In the presence of _____

SIGNED by the above named mentioned _____
(The tenant)

In the presence of _____

Appendix 6

NOTICE OF INTENTION TO SEEK POSSESSION (SECTION 21)

Here is an example of a Section 21 eviction notice:

ASSURED SHORTHOLD TENANCY
NOTICE REQUIRING POSSESSION
(Housing Act, 1988, Section 21 (1) (b))

TO: *[tenant's name]*

OF: *[property address]*

I, *[landlord's name]*

HEREBY give you notice that we require possession of the dwelling house known

AS: *[property address]*

ON: **Monday 22nd September 200X**

or at the end of the period of your tenancy which will end next after a period of two calendar months from the service upon you of this Notice.

DATED: 10th July 200X

SIGNED _____

[landlord's name]

INFORMATION FOR TENANT

1.   If the tenant or licensee does not leave the property, the landlord or licensor must get an order for possession from the court before the tenant or licensee can lawfully be evicted. The landlord or licensor cannot apply for such an order before the Notice to Quit or Notice to Determine has run out.

2.   A tenant or licensee who does not know if he has any right to remain in possession after a Notice to Quit or a Notice to Determine runs out can obtain advice from a solicitor. Help with all, or part, of the cost of legal advice and assistance may be available under the Legal Aid scheme. He should also be able to obtain information from a Citizens' Advice Bureau, a Housing Aid Centre or a rent officer.

NOTES

1. On or after the coming to an end of a fixed term Assured Shorthold Tenancy, a court must make an order for possession if the landlord has given notice in this form.

2. The length of the Notice must be at least two calendar months.

Appendix 7

STANDING ORDER SET UP FORM FOR RENT COLLECTION

Here is an example of standing order set up form for your tenant to complete and hand in to their bank.

Payer

Name:	*Put the tenant's full name here*
Branch:	*Put the tenant's bank branch and full address*
A/C number:	*Put the tenant's account number here*
Sort code:	*Put the tenant's bank branch's sort code*

Payee

Name:	*Put your full name here*
Branch:	*Put your bank branch's name and full address*
A/C number:	*Put your account number here*
Sort code:	*Put your bank branch's sort code here*

Payment details

Amount:	*Put the weekly or monthly rent here*
Transfer date:	*Put the first date you want the transfer to occur here*
Reference:	*Put the address of property here*
Repeat:	*Put the frequency either weekly or monthly here*
Last transfer date:	*Always put **'To be notified in writing'***

Please could you set up the above standing order on my behalf as soon as possible, to ensure that the first transfer payment is paid on time?

_____   _____

Signed Date   Date
(the tenant)

_____

Print Name

Please now send on to the payer's bank branch.

Appendix 8

YIELD PROFIT/CONTRIBUTION TABLE BASED ON YEARS LEFT TO RETIREMENT

YEARS TO RETIREMENT	YIELD 6%	7%	8%	9%	10%	11%	12%
	Retirement income 6,000	7,000	8,000	9,000	10,000	11,000	12,000
	CONTRIBUTION						
5 yrs	−1,236.07	−1,169.40	−1,102.74	−1,036.07	−969.40	−902.74	−836.07
6 yrs	−995.54	−928.87	−862.21	−795.54	−728.87	−662.21	−595.54
7 yrs	−824.14	−757.47	−690.81	−624.14	−557.47	−490.81	−424.14
8 yrs	−695.95	−629.28	−562.62	−495.95	−429.28	−362.62	−295.95
9 yrs	−596.55	−529.88	−463.22	−396.55	−329.88	−263.22	−196.55
10 yrs	−517.32	−450.65	−383.99	−317.32	−250.65	−183.99	−117.32
11 yrs	−452.75	−386.08	−319.42	−252.75	−186.08	−119.42	−52.75
12 yrs	−399.18	−332.51	−265.85	−199.18	−132.51	−65.85	0.82
13 yrs	−354.06	−287.39	−220.73	−154.06	−87.39	−20.73	45.94
14 yrs	−315.59	−248.92	−182.26	−115.59	−48.92	17.74	84.41

15 yrs	−282.42	−215.75	−149.09	−82.42	−15.75	50.91	117.58
16 yrs	−253.58	−186.91	−120.25	−53.58	13.09	79.75	146.42
17 yrs	−228.29	−161.62	−94.96	−28.29	38.38	105.04	171.71
18 yrs	−205.95	−139.28	−72.62	−5.95	60.72	127.38	194.05
19 yrs	−186.11	−119.44	−52.78	13.89	80.56	147.22	213.89
20 yrs	−168.38	−101.71	−35.05	31.62	98.29	164.95	231.62
21 yrs	−152.47	−85.80	−19.14	47.53	114.20	180.86	247.53
22 yrs	−138.12	−71.45	−4.79	61.88	128.55	195.21	261.88
23 yrs	−125.14	−58.47	8.19	74.86	141.53	208.19	274.86
24 yrs	−113.34	−46.67	19.99	86.66	153.33	219.99	286.66
25 yrs	−102.58	−35.91	30.75	97.42	164.09	230.75	297.42
26 yrs	−92.75	−26.08	40.58	107.25	173.92	240.58	307.25
27 yrs	−83.73	−17.06	49.60	116.27	182.94	249.60	316.27
28 yrs	−75.45	−8.78	57.88	124.55	191.22	257.88	324.55
29 yrs	−67.82	−1.15	65.51	132.18	198.85	265.51	332.18
30 yrs	−60.78	5.89	72.55	139.22	205.89	272.55	339.22
Interest Only	45.83	112.50	179.16	245.83	312.50	379.16	445.83

Assumptions: £100,000 purchase price, 85% LTV financing, 5% interest rate, 20% rental income loss and repayment mortgage.

Appendix 9

TOP 5 ANNUITIES FOR MALE, FEMALE AGED 60 AND JOINT LIFE LAST SURVIVOR MALE AGED 60/FEMALE AGED 55
Male Age 60 Annuities – Purchase Price £10k

Company	Level without guarantee (p.a.)	Level guaranteed 5 years (p.a.)	Escalating 5% p.a. compound without guarantee (p.a.)	Notes
Prudential	£630.00	£627.12	£344.40	Minimum purchase price £20k
Legal & General	£627.48	£625.44	£339.84	
Clerical Medical	£617.20	£615.19	£317.29	Minimum purchase price £5k
Scottish Widows	£615.84	£612.60	£328.20	
Standard Life	£612.00	£609.60	£334.80	Minimum purchase price £2k
Canada Life	£611.40	£609.72	£331.80	Minimum purchase price £10k

Female Aged 60 Annuities – Purchase Price £10k

Company	Level without guarantee (p.a.)	Level guaranteed 5 years (p.a.)	Escalating 5% p.a. compound without guarantee (p.a.)	Notes
Prudential	£604.39	£602.54	£308.09	Minimum purchase price £20k
Norwich Union	£594.84	£593.04	£274.44	Minimum purchase price £5k
Scottish Widows	£585.84	£582.72	£288.00	
Legal & General	£585.60	£584.64	£290.04	

Clerical Medical	£581.70	£580.39	£276.79	Minimum purchase price £5k
Canada Life	£579.60	£578.52	£296.64	Minimum purchase price £10k

Joint Life Last Survivor Annuities (male age 60/female age 55) – Purchase Price £10k

Company	Level without guarantee (p.a.)	Level guaranteed 5 years (p.a.)	Escalating 5% p.a. compound without guarantee (p.a.)	Notes
Prudential	£529.30	£529.30	£241.82	Minimum purchase price £20k
Legal & General	£512.52	£512.28	£233.76	
Norwich Union	£511.56	£511.56	£194.84	Minimum purchase price £5k
Clerical Medical	£503.10	£503.10	£209.80	Minimum purchase price £5k
Scottish Widows	£498.36	£497.04	£219.84	
Canada Life	£496.68	£496.68	£225.96	Minimum purchase price £10k

Index